Carolyn,

Sgt. Libby

Charles Libby

Thank you for
Your kindness
to our Warrior for Christ
School, enjoy some
of my work.

God Bless,

Richard Steve Hunter

8-15-2020

Sgt. Libby

100 YEARS OF STORIES

* * *

Steve Hunter

ISBN: 0692956271
ISBN 13: 9780692956274

SGT. LIBBY
100 Years of Stories

WWII TEC5 Sgt. of the 628th Tank Destroyer Battalion C-Company Official M-20 command car driver, Charles A. Libby shares more of his life in this follow up book that acts as the book end to his first paperback entitled, ***From The Command Car.***

Dedication

I would like to thank Sgt. Libby for once again taking the time to share these wonderful stories with me. In started this new project as a follow-up to our first published book entitled, *From The Command Car*, the process seemed to be much easier for the both of us. His friendship and kindness to myself and my family has been a blessing and will never be forgotten. His service through his life is in the stories of these books and his continued efforts to help others is demonstrated to this day in so many ways.

I would also like to thank all of the wonderful people that have sponsored our book events and speeches through the past two years. The response has been overwhelming and the crowds have been full of love, appreciation and admiration for this living hero of both Pennsylvania and world military history! Once again, I thank all of you from the bottom of my heart.

I would also like to thank all the service men and women that sacrificed time away from the comfort of their homes and the love and warmth of their families, some never to return to either of them. This book is dedicated to all of you heroes with heart-filled gratitude and complete admiration.

I would also like to dedicate this to my dad who I lost this year to cancer. It doesn't seem the same for me without the ability to call you and catch up on all the things that are going on in my life, especially on how my writing projects are going. I hope that The Lord is granting you the ability to watch over my shoulder as I type the words of this book and that you are smiling. RIP, Stephen Leroy Hunter — I love and miss you very much *old man*! Our Astros did it!

I would like to thank all of the public and school libraries that house my books on their shelves. It is the ultimate compliment to any author to have his works appreciated and available for all to read. It is my desire that many more make their way into libraries for all to see and enjoy my growing book series which is entitled, *Steve Hunter's Biographical Military Book Series*.

And finally, I would like to thank my Lord and Savior Jesus Christ for his ultimate sacrifice for all of us on the cross so that we may live eternally. Without your love, my journey would be an empty walk through life, void of hope.

Sgt. Libby would like to thank his three children, Chuck, Rob and Debbie as well as Chuck's wife Marilyn, for their love and care they give to him each and every day! He would also like to mention and thank all of the boys from the CCC Camps and the men of his unit, the 628th Tank Destroyer Battalion, for their friendship and memories that have blessed him for so many years. Special mention to General Gallagher and Captain Jones for their influence over him then and to this day.

He would also like to dedicate this book to his late mother and father for all the love they showed him each and every day of their lives. He misses them both greatly!

He wanted everyone to know that this was the story of his life all through the military and his youth. He hopes that all who read it believe him because it is all true. He hopes that everyone enjoys it and always remembers his great unit, the 628th Tank Destroyer Battalion. He feels that his service to America was something that had worth and that his pride in what he did is surely justified.

Acknowledgment

∗ ∗ ∗

At 100 years old, this WWII veteran continues to share the stories of his life to educate others on what he witnessed in war and did throughout his long and blessed life. Sgt. Charles A. Libby is an inspiration and a hero to the many who have read his books *From The Command Car* and now *Sgt. Libby — 100 Years of Stories*.

Table of Contents

Prologue

∗ ∗ ∗

As a child, we looked at an adult having no gauge or value of a way to judge that person's age due to our inexperience in life. We pondered what it will be like to be an adult and be able to make the many choices that will be placed in front of us. We dreamed about our ability to choose what we will do from day-to-day without the consent of our parents and pondered what career path we may choose to pursue. Today, as adults, we look into the eyes of a senior citizen and see the cloudiness that has taken over the bright blue or the deep brown of their once young eyes. For many, this is such an empty and naive way to look deeply into that person and understand what they have seen with those aged eyes over the many years they have lived on this place we call earth.

As we all get older, grow and mature in ourselves, we receive various life lessons through trial and error with the resounding voice of those we looked at as being the old guys or the crazy old lady, realizing that they had once been exactly where we are now. We experience a self-enlightenment, realizing that we should have payed closer attention to them to have avoided the many heartaches which we foolishly placed upon ourselves. We also realize that when we needed that *sage advice*, the person with the cloudy eyes, the weakened legs and the long list of aches and pains is not going to be there any more to help you to sort out life's harder times and complicated decisions.

When a person approaches an age in the triple digits, they receive a certain amount of attention from others based upon their realization of how hard it actually is to reach that milestone in life. They are referred to as a *centenarian,* meaning they are 100+ years old. 100 years of life, 100 years of joys, 100 years of hardships, 100 years of relationships, 100 years of stories and when it comes down to it, 100 years of *survival!* The respect level of that person increases many times over, no matter how old the person trying to comprehend the magnitude of any of these forenamed categories. At this age, you also have the privilege of being mentioned along with such late greats as Bob Hope, George Burns and the still living Kirk Douglas. When this book reaches historians, Sgt. Charles Libby will now be recognized among those important, noteworthy and very recognizable celebrity names.

Now, let us look into the eyes and listen to the words of a man that is not only 100 years old, but one that has also fought in what we referred to as *the war that would end all wars . . .* WWII. A man who defines himself as a *soldier* and served the United States Army in a capacity that few paid much attention to or ever realized how important their particular job was. Never catching the glory like the ACE pilot downing enemy fighter planes or the 4-star General who led his troops into the many victorious battles of the war or the soldier who received a chest full of medals, the command car drivers not only had an awesome responsibility of protecting the officers they drove, but also were required to have nerves of steel while performing their duties day in and day out in the heat of battle. Their hands weren't gripping a weapon, they were placed firmly on a steering wheel attached to an armored vehicle, the M-20 scout command car. With the lives of an officer, a radioman, gunner and himself to keep safe while performing their duty without any hesitations or fear, these drivers deserve attention and special recognition for their many battlefield heroics. They had a job to perform and did not have the luxury of *not knowing* what was about to happen ahead of them. The command car driver heard it all come from HQ by means of the radioman on board his vehicle and *knew* what he was about to face. The officer he drove was needed to direct the many soldiers onto the battlefield and the command car driver needed to get him there quickly. Dodging snipers, landmines, booby-traps, trip wires and incoming artillery, Mr. Libby and other brave and talented drivers of these tank units performed a uniquely specialized and very dangerous job that few people could even imagine doing.

The European Theater of Operations during WWII was a battleground of enemy soldiers that had the tactical advantage of being entrenched for a very long period of time prior to the arrival of US troops. They knew the water and the landscapes and had every opportunity to prepare for the eventual invasion of the Allied Forces. They knew that soldiers and drivers alike would try to reach them along the many rugged and winding paths connecting city to city and did everything they could to hold them up by killing as many as they could with their many deadly traps. Command car drivers who trained in the US on maneuvers within the many forts and camps that were spread across each state prior to their stepping on foreign soil, learned their tactics and with top-flight education and training, these brave men did something that made the difference between a successful driver and one that fell into these traps of the German armies. These boys knew their vehicles, they knew what they were capable of and most of all, they knew how to drive them in a way that any of today's professional racing drivers would most certainly envy!

When reading these newer stories and a few pulled out of *From The Command Car*, feel this spoken history of WWII as witnessed by this official command car driver and keep in mind the many hazards that he faced day-to-day while performing his duties. This book can be treated as either a sequel or a prequel as many stories cross over and recap memories of the first book as well as offering many new and exciting tales from WWII. I will say that it is a bookend and they both need to be read to get the full impact of his wonderful life and his amazing stories! Also remember that these Americans felt deep emotions for all who were fighting there and dreamed every minute of every day about how nice it would be to be back home again with their families. Also remember when reading this newest manuscript that Sgt. Libby is one of the last men of his unit still living. He is one of the last men who witnessed the many battles of WWII and he is also one of the last of the greatest generation of men in American history who enjoyed a life of service and a lifetime of blessings! Enjoy and may God continue to bless Sgt. Charles A. Libby and each one of you.

The Neighborhood

* * *

SGT. LIBBY'S ROOTS GROWING UP in the small town of Williamsport, PA are important to him. His connection with the mountains, the woodlands, the rivers and streams, the streets and buildings as well as the many historical churches and landmarks in this community are still an intricate part of his happiness and the main reason why he still lives there to this very day.

Memories of his childhood friends and what they all did still bring out stories that make him smile. Memories of who he went to school with, who he played with, who was nice to him and who he fell in love with all are fresh within his daily conversations with others. Memories saved in dresser drawers, photo albums and on display surrounding him at his home are all special treasures of the times spent in the old neighborhood.

Charles Libby, age 6 at First Presbyterian Church wall.
Earliest known photo of his childhood.
Photo 1923 unknown photographer.

A once white colored, wavy hair of a young boy matched that of his father's, is now a similar gray that he keeps trimmed and combed back to always look nice for the ladies he dances with regularly. No noticeable age spots on the face, arms or hands like most older veterans carry with them and most all of his own adult teeth still in place. Small hearing aids to help with background noise, no glasses, no use of a cane or walker and eyes that at times in the proper light, sparkle like a diamond. No major operations with all of his organs still in tact at 100 years old so I guess you could say that not much has changed for this man of 100 years.

You can tell in the conversations and in the true mindset of Sgt. Libby that he has not chosen to surrender to the stigma attached to getting old, but rather embrace it and live life to it's fullest through his stories and memories of his days in the old neighborhood, CCC Camp in Benton, Pa and his time serving in WWII.

Frequent reminders about his family come out in the stories he tells me with respect for his mother, father and his grandfather resonating within each word. Lessons taught to him by his father still ring clearly in his ears as he looks at old photos which he has carefully preserved all of these years.

I remember so many things about my younger
years. I remember that my father would scold
me for wiping my nose on my sleeve but he
would also praise me for working hard. I
didn't like that he made me read Little Bo
Peep, but he made me do it to learn how to
read better. He worked very hard and at his
job and I remember that he could hang three
doors to the one that others would hang at
his job. He was both strict and jolly. He
used to carry chestnuts in his pocket to eat
for his rheumatism that helped him with the
pain. He was a good father and a gentleman
and I think of him often . . . C. Libby

**Returned home from combat, Sgt. Libby poses with 2
sisters and his mother and father (center).**
Photo circa 1946, unknown photographer.

He fondly remembers another story of his grandfather and the time that he witnessed a man beating and whipping a helpless horse in the street near his home.

> My grandfather went over to the man, took his whip away and started to beat the man for harming the horse. Another man witnessed what my grandfather had done and approached him about it. Turns out, this man was a boxing promoter and asked my grandfather if he wanted to box and said that he could be a lightweight champion with his help. My grandfather told him no thank you and went on his way. He was a tough man and a very hard worker but did not like seeing that horse getting beat like that . . . C. Libby

A cat named snowball brings back pleasant memories to Sgt. Libby from the old neighborhood. An old faded photo of his furry friend brings a smile to his face, not only because of the cat, but the images of his brother Bob and his sister Naomi captured in the background as well.

> I really liked that cat. She would follow me all around and was really nice. We had it for over five years and one day it got hit by a passing car that didn't even stop to tell us what had happened. We were all very sad . . . C. Libby

One unpleasant, although remarkable, story from his childhood school days is the time that he ran an ice pick into his eye. The young Charles was learning how to properly cane a chair and in the process, he lost control of the ice pick when trying to use his right hand instead of his dominant left hand and ran into his lower left eye just above the skin. It went in far enough that fluid was seeping out of his eye.

> I had a paper route in Williamsport at the time and I had a doctor that I knew on my route. I knocked on the door and told him about what happened and he took me in right away. He said to me, my God boy, get in here! Then he told me that he wanted to look at it and put drops in my eye and told me that if I had waited, I'd of gone blind in that eye. He even called the school and chewed out the teacher for not sending me to him sooner. He saved my eye and I never had any problem after that. He also told me that if I hadn't had gone there, the next day, my eye would be laying on my cheek. I really think that I have had angels watching over me . . . C. Libby

Sgt. Libby had a small procedure in his nineties under that same eye to remove a small section of benign cancer. While examining the eye, the doctor asked him how he got the scar on his eye. Sgt. Libby didn't know that there was a scar on the eye, but told him the story about how it happened. The doctor listened in amazement. Once again, angels watching over this man who does not have to wear eyeglasses to this very day.

A STORY OF HIS CHILDHOOD PULLED OUT OF
THE BOOK *FROM THE COMMAND CAR . . .*
Sgt. Libby recalls some of the more popular games with his neighborhood buddies like playing baseball or sneaking into the local theater to see a free silent movie which at the time would cost five or ten cents while watching a

local resident play the piano while the movie ran. This feature added to the excitement of the film which in turn made up for the fact that it was shown without any sound.

Remembering many of these old films fondly and smiling at the likes of *Charlie Chaplin* and quietly laughing when recalling being scared at films like *The Phantom of The Opera* and *Boris Karloff's Frankenstein* character, Mr. Libby's memories of these times are much like yesterday. *The Keystone Cops* also provided a comical memory as they drove down the road in a sped up motion as the engine dropped right out of the bottom of their car. Following their moment of precise comical timing and unfortunate circumstances, they all get out, picked up the engine, threw it in the back seat and drove off leaving theater goers, like the young Charles Libby, laughing hysterically. He also remembers the first movies that depicted the failed flights of the famous *Wright Brothers*. Snickering about the planes flipping over and the footage of how they kept trying before they finally succeeded, Mr. Libby proudly remarks that he saw the history of flight from the very start and then eventually a man being blasted into space. Charles was fortunate to be living in a unique generation of rapid growth and technological advancements that only a man of his advanced age would have had the chance to see and experience.

Other favorite childhood activities were hiking up Bald Eagle Mountain as well as hanging out by the local dam and various swimming holes. Being strong and brave enough to swim completely across the wide Susquehanna River at one clip, Charles takes pride in the fact that he was always in great shape and took great care of his body. As a child, Charles recalls that he knew the river's currents well enough to help emergency rescue teams find a young boy who had drown in some of its rougher waters. While these rescue teams where looking for a young boy out in the center area of the river, young Charles instructed the many volunteers and rescue personal to search in a particular area where they were able to find the lifeless body from his exact instructions. Just a start of the long line of remarkable and unselfish deeds that Sgt. Libby would speak about while being interviewed for this manuscript.

More from his school days, Sgt. Libby recalls his very first love, Ann Dailey. He recalls everything about her and tells me of his school boy crush and their private meetings during those times.

```
We would meet under the chestnut tree near
our home and sit in the shadows of the
branches, kissing and hugging like children
do. Nothing bad, just innocent kissing and
enjoying each others company like kids did
in those days . . . C. Libby
```

He remembers an angry man coming out and yelling at the two to get away from that chestnut tree or he would call the police. Innocent fun stopped by an angry neighbor. He also fondly remembers how he got even with the man over his threats with a popular childhood prank.

```
Halloween came around and I went to
Montoursville, PA where they would butcher
cattle. I had a wooden spoon and a bucket
and filled the bucket with cow manure. One
night when nobody was home and the porch
light wasn't on, I went onto his porch and
up to his door and smeared the manure on
the knob of the door,, then on the landing
and then on the first step of the porch. I
didn't stick around to see what happened af-
ter that, but I sure fixed him . . . C. Libby
```

When the young Charles went to the CCC Camp to work, his first true love married a man who himself joined the US Navy. While in the Navy, he shot himself, leaving Ann a widow. Sgt. Libby remembers how badly he felt for her and they quickly became good friends once again after his return home in 1936.

Living in this particular town during the days of the depression, Williamsport had it's share of immigrants that settled there for jobs and to start families from Russia, Poland, Ireland, Scotland and Italy. Charles made friends with all the different kids and enjoyed their cultures and the rich heritage and traditions of each one.

Mr. Bragalone and Mr. Dominick are two Italian men that made quite an impression on him at an early age. They would always be outside working in their gardens and would wave and say hello to the young Irish kid from the neighborhood walking by on his way to work.

```
One day, Mr. Bragalone was sitting on his
porch and saw me walking by. It was near
Christmas time and they had wine they made
themselves. He said to me, Charlie, you come
in and have a drink with me. To me, to be
invited into his house was an honor that not
many others were treated to. We sat and had
a sip or two of wine together and he talked
to me like a friend. I really liked him and
all the other Italians that I made friends
with from the neighborhood . . . C. Libby
```

IN *FROM THE COMMAND CAR*, I COVERED HIS CHILDHOOD EXTENSIVELY. HERE'S A TRUE GEM.
Charles also remembers from his youth the *Black Hand Gang,* who ran most of the city's underground and illegal operations during these hard times by making moonshine and selling their highly desired liquor out the back door of the local theater and many other local businesses within the city of Williamsport.

Being egged-on by his neighborhood buddies to try and get them a bottle of whiskey, Mr. Libby remembers knocking on one of those doors with only twenty five cents in his pocket which they all scraped together for this *hail marry* attempt at getting some moonshine alcohol.

During prohibition, a black market bottle of whiskey would cost interested parties fifty cents. Now, here was a young Charles Libby, of Irish decent, knocking on a door in a dark alley of the notorious Italian *Black Hand Gang*, trying to buy whiskey for young boys and only having half of the amount that was being demanded at that time. Mr. Libby recalls that he knocked at the door and boldly told the man that he knew what was going on there and that he would tell the local cops about them, *unless* he could buy a fifth of whiskey. The large man that had opened the door looked down at the cocky young Irish boy and told him that he was a little brat, as he attempted to close the door in his face. As Charles quickly stuck his foot in the doorway, the now panicking man frantically told him to get his foot out of the doorway.

Mr. Libby still remembers with a big smile on his face the moment that he was looking at this man once again and telling him that he would tell the cops if he didn't sell him the whiskey that he and his neighborhood friends wanted. Reluctantly, the man had no other choice and was forced to open the door and allow the young and bold Charles to enter. Knowing that their entire operation was at stake of being ratted out by a twelve year old boy, the man reluctantly sold Charles a pint of whiskey, at his requested discounted price. After that, all the other neighborhood boys knew that if they wanted to get booze from the Black Hand Gang, Charles was the guy to get it for them, but for a price of course. This was just one of the ways that Charles took those desperate times and turned it into a small enterprising business operation to help out his family, as well as having some of his own spending money in his pocket for candy and the movies.

Sounds like something right out of a Little Rascals episode with a slightly rated R twist. As time went on and trust was built between this notorious gang and Charles, he sometimes acted as a lookout for their illegal operations. He remembers the times of alerting them to the police passing by and then giving the all clear to the men as they were far enough away to resume their underground booze business during this time of prohibition. With one of those grins on his face, he takes a moment to tuck the story back into his memories and moves right along into the next tale of his childhood with the comment of . . .

```
They didn't have a choice of selling me the
booze. I was young and hard-headed. Whatever
I wanted as a kid, I knew that I was going
to try hard and would get it . . . C. Libby
```

SGT. LIBBY — 100 YEARS OF STORIES . . .

In preparing to finish up this book and try to add as many stories and as much information about his upbringing and his blessed 100 years, on his 100th birthday I took him to take the photos that placed him in front of the same spot the he was photographed at the age of six. During our photo sessions and our many conversations, he then pointed to the end of the church and told me that his house used to be just around the corner. I walked with him around the corner of the old stone building and the memories of those days gone by started to flood him with fond and happy memories. He walked me to the very spot that the house stood all those years ago and began to survey the area, pointing out to me the various landmarks that would had been there in the 1920's through the 1940's.

```
Right here stood my house that I lived in
as a child and into my days after returning
home from the war before I moved on my own.
I can still see the house, the shrubbery and
everything that surrounded our property.
That was so long ago . . . C. Libby
```

During our visit to this spot, a woman from inside the church came out as she overheard us talking about the property. She quickly asked for his last name and his father's as well so that she could start to research the old deeds that the church had on file. You could see the face of Sgt. Libby beaming with pride as he recited his father's name to her. He is very proud of his family and his upbringing and enjoys sharing the stories with all who will listen.

```
I remember playing hide and seek with the
neighborhood boys. I used to hide in a ledge
of a window on the church that I could climb
into where they never found me. I remember
one time I climbed in there and as it became
dark, I looked out and had two glowing eyes
staring back at me. I believed at the time
that they were the eyes of the devil star-
ing at me! I climbed out and got my buddies
to come and try to see what I did, but none
of them could see the same thing. It scared
me and I never used that spot again when we
played hide and seek. I can still see those
eyes in my head to this very day . . . C.
Libby
```

So when the questions of war and what was about to happen on the other side of the world came into our many conversations and what he thought as a child, his answers were simple and direct in this particular interview session . . .

Sgt. Libby, did you practice or have drills for air raids? The response, *No!* Sgt. Libby, didn't your mom and dad think about what would happen if planes or bombs started to enter your skies and what would happen to you and your family? The response, *No! They were too far away to hurt us here. They couldn't fly that far, we thought about any of them.* Sgt. Libby, was your mom worried about the war? The response, *Yes! Her brother, my Uncle Lyman was in WWI and she knew what he had done and had seen. She worried about anoth-er world war and kept quiet about it. No drills, no talk about it, we just went about our lives and did what we had to do.* Sgt. Libby, did you follow what was going on via the radio to hear about the Germans taking over other countries? The response, *No! We were too busy trying to stay alive and feed our family. We were all trying to find work and stay warm in the winters.* Sgt. Libby, when did you really realize that there was something wrong over there and that you needed to do something? The response, *I guess it was during my time in the CCC Camps and the time the Japanese bombed Pearl Harbor. Then I knew that I was probably going to be in the military and doing the same thing my Uncle Lyman did just a short time before me.*

As a writer, I often have to say to myself . . . *enough!* There has to be a point that I trust that I have given my subject all that it needs for a reader to understand it and to completely fall in love with it at the same time. That is so hard to do when you have a subject like Sgt. Charles Libby. His stories just keep going on and on and on . . .

I caught myself wondering about his complete dedication to his family, meaning his mother and father, and all that he did to provide for them. I wondered when exactly he moved out of their home for good and made it on his own. As I do often, I picked up the telephone and called him to ask a simple question, "*When did you move out on your own?*"

```
It wasn't until after I married my wife
Virginia that I finally moved out on my
own. I rented a few different places before
settling on the home that I still live in
today with my son. It was around 1949 when
I married her and started my family. We had
a very small ceremony with just a couple of
people present . . . C. Libby
```

**First purchased home of Charles Libby with family members
– Left to right : Virginia Libby, Charles Libby, Theodore Libby,
Uncle Lyman, children – Chuck, Deb and Rob Libby.**
Photo circa 1962, unknown photographer.

As our childhood quickly passes and we look back in our advanced years to those days, we start to realize how it shaped us. We realize that the time we spent without worries or without the many factors of life that clutter our minds, were the best times ever. A 100 year old WWII veteran shares these vivid memories with a man who is half his age in an effort to not only pass on and preserve the memories of his family and childhood, but also lends them to me for my own use in my own life. He offers them to me as a gift that he paid for with time, laughs, blood, sweat and tears. I gladly accept these many gifts, the many stories and will use them for both my benefit and my enjoyment in those moments of solitude and self-reflection. For the wisdom of the ones who precede us never wrinkles, it never weakens and it never passes away like the bodies we use to achieve the knowledge we share to others.

CCC Boys America's Forgotten Heroes!

* * *

THE CCC CAMPS ACROSS THE United States during the great depression served as a way to not only employ young boys to help their families survive financially, they also served as a proving ground for what *life itself* was about to throw at them as young adults. In a time of world instability at the brink of war, The **Civilian Conservation Corps** enacted by President Franklin D. Roosevelt blended a military presence and the know-how of skilled forestry engineers to blaze through the roughest of terrain in many areas of our great country. Trees needed to be cut down, rocks needed to be blasted through, debris needed to be moved, bridges needed to be built, highways needed to go through these rugged areas of forest and our hard-working American boys met these challenges with success while receiving the love, respect and admiration of the entire country!

Entrance to CCC Camp Morton in Benton, PA.
Photo circa 1934, photographer unknown.

With the many camps being established and the many young men being accepted into this wonderful program, hope seemed to be satisfied both financially and skill-based. As these boys not only provided important money for their family, they also were given valuable knowledge that would help to give them the proper skill sets which would lift them above many others in the troubling job markets of those hard times. These boys would also adapt so well to the discipline of these camps due to their military supervision that many would see either a long career or at least a basic four year stint in the many branches of the US armed forces. To aid in this great cause that our country was facing across the oceans in the Pacific, North-African and European Theaters of Operations, a young Charles Libby was one of those boys that found the lifestyle appealing and wanted not only to aid in the fighting, but also looked forward to the excitement of what he may find in one of these foreign lands that he had only seen and heard about until then in his early school books, magazines and the local newspaper.

In our first book working together, entitled *From The Command Car*, Sgt. Libby spoke of the many things the boys were required to do on a daily basis. He spoke of the hard work, the men who were in charge of them, the many activities they participated in at the camp and the great times he had before being asked to leave the program and return home to help his father in the clean up effort of their family home following a destructive flood in the Williamsport, PA area. In more recent conversations, Sgt. Libby recalls even more stories to share with readers about what they did, saw and experienced during those times to provide further insight into the day-to-day life of a CCC boy.

During our many appearances speaking on the first book, many people had a great interest in these camps due to their family members working in them or living near an area that used to house one of these important work camps. Sgt. Libby provides a look into some aspects of the camps and satisfies the desire to hear about what their fathers, uncles or other family members did during their time spent working in one. Expressed to me as a great experience, Sgt. Libby smiles while reflecting back on those days gone by and tells me that he loved working there, made many great friends and that he would have returned if the camps had stayed open into his later years after returning home from the war. This is a true testament of how much it affected and shaped him in his early years of age.

On Facebook, visit the page called : **Civilian Conservation Corps Legacy** and see the discussions that many are having about this rich and almost forgotten history. Join the group and share any family memories and information that you may have about a CCC Boy to help preserve this great American legacy for many years to come.

A QUICK CCC STORY PULLED OUT OF *FROM THE COMMAND CAR* . . .
With five large barracks in this particular camp that young Charles was stationed in and approximately sixty boys to a barrack, each of these boys would

work for a rate of five dollars per month for the young man to keep for his own use and a rate of twenty five dollars per month to be sent back to their family at home. This amount of money that the United States Government paid for participating was certainly a blessing to the many who were accepted within this valuable program.

```
You either worked or you were told to get
out, pack your bags and go home. They didn't
fool around when it came to that. This was
hard work and nobody loafed on the job! . . .
C. Libby
```

These barracks became the young boy's new home. Living there full time and all donning military green fatigues as their type of uniforms, the young men lived a strict lifestyle enjoying it all the while. The other option, *starving*, seemed like a senseless route to take with their lives. So, the hard work became routine and a blessing to all of those who were fortunate to be a part of a CCC Camp during those tough economic times. Hot of the summer or cold of the winter, the boys all did their assigned jobs with pride. The satisfaction of knowing that their hard work was lifting a great financial burden from their beloved families back home wherever that may have been gave them pride.

AND THE CCC STORIES CONTINUE . . .

6:30 AM bugle call at Camp Morton in Benton, PA. Two boys bring a folded American flag out to raise on the camp's flag pole as the other boys are rustled up by the 1st Sgt. to get dressed with a hammering on the door, "*Come on guys, let's go!*" A quick making of their beds and out the door to report for roll call in the camp's courtyard. For the one's that didn't hear the morning ruckus, covers get pulled off as a little more incentive is initiated by the sergeant to make sure they are up and ready for the day's full and rigorous schedule of work activities.

For the boys, out to the courtyard, line up in formation and get ready for a military style roll call. When you heard your name announced, the boys would yell their last name back at the person taking role. When finished, back to the barracks to check the *Day's Advisory Bulletin Board* to see what they will be involved with for the day by finding your name attached to that function. This would also determine how you would dress for that day. A fatigue hat, overalls and your ankle boots if you were going to work on the dynamite crew or proper dress clothes if the day involved going somewhere outside of the camp and if necessary, the Sgt. would tell you what to wear. Then, off to the mess hall for a big and hearty breakfast. All the boys always ate well at these camps according to Mr. Libby.

```
They wanted to make sure that we had plenty
of energy when we went out to work on the
job. We usually ate fried eggs, hot cakes,
toast, creamed dried beef over toast, bacon
and beans cooked in some form of syrup.
Lunch was delivered to you at the work site
which consisted of a peanut butter sand-
wich, fig newton cookies and water or co-
coa in a canteen depending on the season.
Supper usually consisted of sauerkraut, hot
dogs, mashed potatoes, hamburgers and on
Thanksgiving we had a big turkey dinner
which was really good! We all knew when they
blew chow call to get to the mess hall, even
the small bear cubs that we found in a tree
trunk one time and brought back to the camp,
knew that they would be fed by the cook when
they heard that sound . . . C. Libby
```

The camp itself had all the amenities for a comfortable stay during a boy's stint in a CCC Camp. Comfortable barracks, beds were army cots that had a comfortable pillow and mattress for a good night of sleep, lighted roads throughout the camp, a swimming hole the boys made themselves, a recreation hall, a big chow house and the PX (*post exchange*) where the boys would be able to purchase items like candy and chocolate bars with peanuts in them.

> I liked the camp and remember every building and everything about them even to this day. I remember that the recreation hall had a big rooster weather vein on top of it that the blacksmith made. One day the wind tore it off. I always found it to be very interesting. Sad, they never did put it back on the roof . . . C. Libby

In my interviews with Sgt. Libby, I try to present him with thought provoking questions that may spark additional stories that I can use to provide more information as to what the days of the CCC Camps were really like and how the boys changed and adapted to this new lifestyle. Within these many questions, I asked a simple one that led me to understand a little more about these unsung and almost forgotten young heroes.

My question was simple, what did you carry in your pockets? The answer was just as simple but showed me this . . . they were still boys. They were helping their families, they were working hard, they were placed in a military style environment, but at the beginning and the end of each day, they were all still boys. So as the question was presented to Mr. Libby, he still remembers this as if it were yesterday. . . *"Sgt. Libby, when you were in the CCC Camps, what did you carry in your pockets?"*

> I carried my pocket watch and some marbles. I really didn't need to carry much because everything we needed was provided to us at that time . . . C. Libby

I then asked, *"Marbles, why marbles?"* The response was equally justified by it's simplicity, which brought me great pleasure as both a friend and a writer and brought a big smile to my face.

```
When I was younger, I used to be pretty good
at playing marbles and I used to like looking
at all the different colors . . . C. Libby
```

Boys doing the work of men, efficiently and done properly, but the reminder within the front pocket of the pants of a man that would soon be asked to drive officers into battle half way across the world, was a subtle reminder that deep down in his heart, he was still a boy wishing to play marbles in the alley with his buddies from the neighborhood. Never to forget exactly why he was where he was and why he was doing what he was doing. He was there to help the family that he loved and cared about and to help provide a better life for them with that income he was earning.

In further questions about the camp itself, the recreation hall seemed to be one of the favorite places for the boys to be since they were permitted to play sports, dance and perform other physical activities. It also acted as the place where the boys would get their physicals from the nurses that would visit from the Bloomsburg Hospital on a regular basis. If someone was injured and needed some more immediate attention but didn't need to be transported to the hospital itself, the recreation hall would be their makeshift exam room.

The blacksmith building of Camp Morton is another of his fond memories. An old farmer ran that building named Jim Crossmore. He worked on tools that needed repaired for the road crews at the camp and any other odd jobs that a maintenance man or blacksmith would perform.

```
He was a very nice man and we became pretty
good friends. He stayed with us during the
```

week and would go home on the weekends. He loaned me his 16 gauge shotgun and would ask me to go and shoot some rabbits for him to eat and I would gladly help him out. I remember to this day how he instigated something of a trick we played on one of the foreman there. I told him that I found some Limburger cheese that Earl Bender had hidden between some extra blankets in storage. Earl was a short and chubby guy that the other foreman didn't really like too much. He was kind of cocky and they didn't like that about him. As a joke to play on him, Mr. Crossmore asked me to go to the kitchen and try to find some bread and then bring that cheese over as well. I did it and we sat and had a sandwich laughing the entire time. I slid the cheese back into it's hiding place, what was left and we never said a word. Later that week, he found the half-eaten cheese and said if I ever find anyone taking my cheese, someone's gonna get hurt. He moved it to the other side of the blanket storage and I found it again. This time, we had a sandwich, but didn't take as much as we did the time before. When he found it missing again he told me that he wasn't gonna buy any more. He never found out that it was me and the blacksmith that ate it. We used to have a lot of fun together . . . C. Libby

Many other names came up during the interviews of people that had an impact on Sgt. Libby including Mr. Potter. This man was over the other foreman of the camp and was personally in charge of the bridge building projects that the CCC Camps did so well.

> I remember that he was a very nice man and knew what he was doing! He would come in after our dynamite crew was finished and build the small bridges that needed to be built. I spoke to someone many years back and they told me that the bridge Mr. Potter was in charge of building between Jefferson City and Red Rock was still standing after all those years. I don't know if it is still there today, but it sure lasted a very long time . . . C. Libby

A variety of clothing was provided to each boy at every CCC camp. Sgt. Libby recalls some of the clothing that they all had at their disposal like their work overalls, a blue fatigue hat, protective rain gear, ankle high work boots and winter boots they referred to as arctics.

> They always made sure that we were protected from the cold and that we had good clothes to do our work in. They always took good care of us . . . C. Libby

Sgt. Libby also fondly recalls the games that the boys would play within the camp as well with other camps in the areas near Benton, PA. Friendly competitions between the camps in sports such as swimming meets, baseball games and basketball tournaments were all favorites of these strong and competitive boys.

> We were all respectful with one another and there was no fighting between the camps at

```
all. We were there to learn and help out the
community, not to fight them. We enjoyed
the games and enjoyed meeting some of the
other CCC boys . . . C. Libby
```

Sgt. Libby does recall just a few times, very rarely, that tensions got high from the stress of the long days and a couple of the CCC boys ended up fighting within his camp.

```
We surrounded them so that they could fin-
ish it and get it over and out of their
system. We made a square block much like a
boxing ring and they fought it out. When
it was over, they shook hands and everyone
got back to their own business. We weren't
supposed to be fighting so nobody ever said
a thing about it to any of the officers in
charge . . . C. Libby
```

Dancing was the one activity that young Libby enjoyed the most! Being that the camps were all boys, you had to suck it up and learn the dance moves and practice with each other. A boy with the last name of Maggs was Libby's dance partner most often at the camp. Sgt. Libby recalls that Maggs was a really nice guy, had a muscular build and became his good friend during those times. Once a month, girls were permitted to enter the camp and they would hold a dance in the recreation hall. They would also travel to other camps as well to a bigger event that was held in Berwick, PA once every three months. The well-known *Hi-Tri Dance* would cost the boys .65 each and if a well-known *big band* was there, the dance would cost them $1.65 to enter and participate in the fun. With a big grin on his face and half laughing while telling the story to me, Sgt. Libby shares one about how the boys used to try to sneak by the men in charge of the camp.

> Sometimes, we'd try to hide girls under the
> bench seats of the trucks to take them back
> to our camp. We'd always get caught after
> the men inspected them to make sure that we
> were all on board to head back to the camp.
> But, we tried . . . C. Libby

Harmless fun for some of these boys that worked so hard to provide for their families as well as performing the hard labor that was so vital to our country. These dances were great for morale and in the case of Charles Libby, they provided him with a lifelong passion and way to stay young and fit!

Charles also knew that learning how to dance and to do it well would help him in meeting young ladies. So, anytime that they had the chance to practice, they did just that.

> When we left the camp to go and dance, we
> were all to be dressed like gentleman. We
> wore our pressed uniforms and acted accord-
> ingly. It was very important that we acted
> like gentleman and that we didn't do any-
> thing to shame the camp. When we'd arrive
> at the camp we were going to dance at, the
> man in charge would say to us, okay fellas,
> go get em' and fellas, be a gentleman! . . .
> C. Libby

To this day, his dancing skills and the way he dresses both get compliments from others around him and on the dance floors he frequents each week. Yes, even at 100 years old, he stills goes dancing and uses the entire floor to move freely with his partner. Others sit in awe and watch him glide across the floor with the ladies like he has done for the past 85 years all over the US. His body may be getting tired, but when on the dance floor, the aches and pains disappear and he becomes that young man who learned so much about dancing within these CCC Camps for which we honor and remember.

Being that the camps were all men and no women, the ability to monitor the boys and their activities was an easier task. They were specific times where they allowed visitors in the camp. Sunday was designated as visitors day for the boys. This is the day that friends and family could pay him a visit and spend some quality time with them to see how they was doing.

```
There was a sign at the camp entrance say-
ing that guests could only come there on
Sunday. It was nice to see everyone enjoying
their company that day. My family never came
to see me because I would get permission to
leave every now and then on a Sunday to go
home to visit them and all I had to do was
to be back early Monday morning. The camp
also provided us with the Sunday paper for
us to catch up on the news and read the fun-
nies of the time like Jiggs, Old Molly and
Flapper Fanny. I really liked to read those
when I was young . . . C. Libby
```

Down the road from Camp Morton, there was a Protestant Church that the boys could visit on their own if they chose to. Sgt. Libby recalls that some of the boys would attend before their family would come to visit them for the day. They were always glad for the boys to attend and all were welcome.

Sgt. Libby also recalls that some of the boys had their own cameras and would take photos of themselves with their families during the visit. In fact, many of these boys provided young Charles with copies of the pictures that he still has today and were used in our first book as well as this one of the camp itself! Capturing these camps in photos didn't seem as important back then to a young boy, but now, these photo are like gold to those who desire to see into the past and into the life of the camps and the boys themselves.

I wanted to know more about personal choices and the rules and goings on of the camp and asked the question about the boys being permitted to smoke while working at the camp.

We were all allowed to, but not too many did. A few would from time to time, but not too many. I did see a guy that chewed snuff and had done it for a very long time. He pulled his lip back one time to show me where he would put it and you could see the bone under his teeth with no skin left from doing it for so long. It was a terrible thing to see and he just smiled like it was nothing. I stayed away from that stuff and only smoked for a very short time during the war but stopped. I found that I could make money by selling my cigarettes they gave us to the other soldiers and other civilians in Europe that I met which was healthier for me anyhow. I made about ten dollars a carton selling them to the Belgians and British people . . . C. Libby

I often asked Sgt. Libby about some of the things that created trouble for all of the boys while working their long days in the woods. Most commonly, he would speak of the long and cold winters of Pennsylvania and how they all had to prevent from getting frost bite. Rattlesnakes were also a problem between Red Rock and Jefferson City in the dense woods. While working on blasting rocks, they were commonly seen slithering through the downed trees and stumps or sunning themselves on rocks where the boys had to work. Often, the snakes were hard to see until you got right up on them. As you can imagine, this was a hazard and potentially deadly if a boy was to get bitten by one of these highly poisonous rattlers. According to Sgt. Libby, they often would see them on their job sites and never payed much attention to them unless they were really close to them.

```
I remember one time, myself and the dyna-
mite crew were riding in the truck to go to
the site for more rock blasting. One of the
guys was looking off to the side and yelled
that there was a rattlesnake right where we
were going to be working sunning in plain
view. Another guy said, one of us could get
bitten if we don't kill it. He looked at
me and said, Charlie, you get off and go
kill that snake. You are the only one brave
enough to go and do it. So, I jumped off
the truck and walked down below the snake
as it was coiled up on a rock sunning it-
self. I picked up a huge flat, heavy rock
and moved closer to the rattlesnake for my
one chance. I could barely lift the rock it
was so heavy. I got close enough and dropped
it right on the snake's head and it never
moved again. I guess I managed to kill it
and protect the others from getting bitten
that day . . . C. Libby
```

The CCC Camp at the end of a day . . . The foreman of each of the barracks would make sure at the end of each night that all were accounted for and that lights were out at 11:00 PM. Being that their days were so long and the work was hard, the boys were all too ready for bed. After supper, just before the boys would be done for the night and Charles being the foreman's orderly, he would go and check to see if any of the foreman would need anything done before lights out. His chores required for him to make sure that the ashes were cleaned from the fireplace, their shoes were clean and shined, their linens were attended to and a few other requested duties that he would perform for them.

Sgt. Libby also recalls that before bed many of the boys would play cards and some of them would even shot craps, a dice gambling game. One boy liked to read quietly quite a bit and would keep to himself in the barracks at night while reading his books on Douglas Fairbanks and others about the history and happenings of WWI. As in any group of boys, there is always one that finds a way to pick on or antagonize the quiet ones. One such a guy taunted this CCC boy each and every night about his reading and about the fact that he didn't participate in the card and craps games that the others were playing. He would refer to this boy as *Tit Willey* for some odd reason, but never got under the skin of the avid reader. The other boys stayed out of it for the most part until one night, my buddy and dance partner Maggs had enough of the teasing and taught the teaser a lesson.

```
Maggs went over to the guy and told him that
he was to stop teasing the kid and leave
him alone. The guy mouthed off and Maggs
hauled off and punched him in the mouth.
He hit him so hard that he flew across the
room and slid on the floor getting his head
stuck under a furnace frame. Us boys all
hurried over to help him get out before one
of the barracks leaders or a camp foreman
came into our barracks from all the commo-
tion. The kid was scared to death that he
was going to cut his own throat on the metal
of that frame. All of us boys helped to lift
```

```
the frame and slide him out of that mess. He
never teased that kid again. Problem solved
and we were all back to our card games and
the quiet one went back to his reading,
never to be teased again. I was glad that it
ended for him because I really liked that
fella . . . C. Libby
```

And now for an embarrassing story about a young Charles Libby from the CCC Camp to make you smile. One day the boys decided that a *snapping the towel fight* in the shower was in order. Charles got a really good one in on one of the boys named Joe Bradley that almost opened up the skin on his backside. There was a huge red mark left behind from the towel that everyone could see. Joe decided to get some sweet revenge on the now laughing Charles Libby. He walked over to Charles and grabbed a handful of his manhood! Yes, you read it right, his manhood. Charles, in shock and in some very serious pain at that moment, froze in his tracks. The other boy had already placed a towel around his naked body and proceeded to walk Charles out of the shower and into the camp courtyard. He paraded him through the entire camp, stark naked and fearing for the safety of his future children! Joe didn't let go until enough people had seen Charles in his *full glory* throughout the entire camp.

```
I didn't know what to do. It hurt really bad
and he had a tight enough grip on me that
I had to follow him and really couldn't do
anything about it. He held on until he got
me to the PX and then finally he let go.
Then, I had to get back to the showers,
still completely naked and get my clothes
on. I never snapped Joe again with a towel,
I learned my lesson,, the hard way! . . .
C. Libby
```

As he tells the story now, he laughs and recalls all the fun they had during their down time. The friends he made, the experiences both good and embarrassing as well as all that he learned from this camp, still flood his memories today. A proving ground in many ways for young men to gain a real- world education and prepare them for their time they would spend in the armed forces protecting our country and fighting against a horrible menace that was spreading across Europe. A wonderful program that is an important aspect of our American history that should be celebrated and never lost. More importantly, a program with a rich history that should continue today for those who need work and can fill these types of jobs to help balance out our many government assistance programs and give them a sense of worth as they help and get helped at the same time. The true American spirit of hard work, ethics and appreciation of what we have gained and how far we have come as a nation, lives in the stories of these camps. A special thanks to all the boys and men that served in this capacity long ago.

ANOTHER GREAT CCC STORY PULLED OUT
OF *FROM THE COMMAND CAR* . . .

Another service which young Charles was proud to have had a part in was saving the life of a young girl who lived near the CCC Camp. This young girl who lived locally in Benton, PA, had come into her time of maturing as a young lady. The flow of blood was too great from her body and she became very weak and in desperate need for blood to help to save her life. Later in life, doctors determined that a rare disease had also contributed to her rapid blood loss. The local hospital desperately needed to find the correct blood type of AB positive to provide her with an urgent blood transfusion. One of the nurses attending to this young girl recommended to her family that they go to the local CCC Camp to see if there was a qualified donor to help in this serious emergency.

An announcement was made to the boys at the evening meal by Captain Jack Thompson. He told all the boys that there was a girl who was going to die unless someone could step up and help her out by providing blood for the necessary life-saving transfusion. After the meal, twenty seven of the boys went to where the medical staff was attending to the girl at her home to see who would be the correct donor type. Upon arrival, all twenty seven of these boys waited outside for their turn to get their blood type matched. While waiting their turn, Sgt. Libby remembers that the boys all laid in the grass on this nice day in the month of May. After the completion of the testing, the attending nurse came outside and announced to all of the boys, "*Which one of you boys is Charlie Libby?*" Charles replied that he was that boy and the nurse anxiously told him that they would take him in first. As he walked into the room and saw the young girl, Mr. Libby remarked that she already looked as if she was dead from her pale white skin color and the stillness of her ailing and frail body.

Dr. Snyder, who was in charge of her treatment, told young Charles that he would be taking his blood directly from his arm and putting it straight into hers. It had to be done quickly and there was no time for any other known medical methods of transfusions. Mr. Libby remembers this transfusion procedure like it was yesterday and recalls every single detail of this crude but effective procedure . . .

```
She was actually coming back to life! They
took a pint and three quarters from me be-
cause she really needed it. That is more
than they would usually take from any one
person, but I didn't mind if it was going
to help to save her life. I was glad that I
could be the one to help her . . . C. Libby
```

After completing the life-saving mission, the doctor told the nurse, "*Take this boy down to the kitchen, give him two shots of whiskey first, a quart of milk and a cheese sandwich and make sure he eats it all.*" Mr. Libby also remembers that they had offered each of the boys twenty five dollars to go and help out this ailing girl. He added more about the money offer during this conversation . . .

```
At first, I thought it would be a great way
to send my mother and father an extra $25.
But afterward, I forgot all about the money
that they offered me and never asked for
it. Everybody else forgot about it as well
because it was the right thing to do . . .
C. Libby
```

Everybody loaded back into the truck and headed back to the camp with a true sense of personal satisfaction knowing that they had all just done something good, especially the young AB positive donor Charlie Libby. Although the other boys on the truck didn't match the ailing girl's blood, they too had the opportunity to donate for others who were in need at the time and many did so.

The boys of the camps would be given weekend passes from time to time and Charles was always ready and willing to get back home to see his family. One particular weekend, Charles was headed home, via hitchhiking, and almost made it there only to be asked to come back due to the declining health once more of this young Seward girl. Captain Jack was urgently alerted by the medical staff that she would need some more of Charlie's blood because it had worked before whereas another boy's blood type had not met her medical needs. The captain asked the others in the camp where they thought Charles would be at that time. They all determined that he would be somewhere at the foot of the North Mountain by then on his return to the camp. Captain Jack himself drove over the mountain in a brand new Hudson to find this much needed blood donor. Mr. Libby remembers the event as such . . .

```
I remember that he screeched to a halt scar-
ing me from the hurried stop. He looked at
me and asked, Are you Charlie Libby? I said,
yes sir, I am. Captain Jack told me that I
was going to have to go and give that girl
another transfusion due to her bleeding too
```

```
much once again. He drove me to the girl
and I was asked to give another full pint
of blood. The transfusion helped the young
girl almost immediately and I felt good
about what I had done for her once again. I
could see her color coming back as my blood
went into her arm. It was as if all of her
energy was back in her body and she actually
looked much better . . . C. Libby
```

After the transfusion, Charles went into the kitchen of the house. Mr. Seward, the young girl's father, came down to speak with Charles and told him, "*Charlie, if I had a million dollars, I would share it with you.*" He then asked Charles to go back to the young girl because she wanted to see him privately before he left to go back to the CCC Camp. With a cracking within his voice Mr. Libby emotionally commented that while she was laying there in the bed he vividly remembers each and every thing about her improved condition.

```
I could not believe how much she had im-
proved! She smiled and talked to me, shook
my hand as she thanked me for the second
blood transfusion. Her color was much better
and it seemed that she had some life back
in her . . . C. Libby
```

Approximately ten years later, Sgt. Libby told me that he contacted her father after finding his telephone number in the phone book. He wanted to see how this girl was doing that he had helped long ago and how everything had turned out with her health. Her father indicated that she had gotten married and that she had three girls of her own. Still appreciative and happy to have heard from Charles, he was still very fond of him and his great gift that he provided to save his precious daughter's life. Sgt. Libby still feels that this act of kindness may be one of the reasons that God has given him such a long, healthy, productive and blessed life.

To hear another exciting and heart-warming twist in this particular story, you'll have to read *From The Command Car* on pages 39-41 and be touched even more about this amazing mans life of service and lifetime of blessings.

Sgt. Libby's blood donations continued far into his later years donating over 12 gallons of blood to the American Red Cross. This is something that he is very proud of and talks about it often to others about how important it is to donate blood for others to save lives.

```
I have AB Positive blood which is very rare.
If they needed it, I was happy to give it to
them to save lives. Over 12 gallons I gave
to The Red Cross in my younger days and I'd
gladly do it again if needed . . . C. Libby
```

Recently at a book signing event, Sgt. Libby was awarded a pin from CCC Camp Legacy organization which honors the remaining men from the CCC Camps. A representative, John Eastlake presented this pin to Sgt. Libby and he was very excited to have been recognized due to his special connection and love for these camps, especially Camp Morton of Benton, PA.

Forest fires were another chore for the boys of the CCC Camps to tackle. In recent conversation with Sgt. Libby, I asked him about the mountain fires and what their role was when they occurred near the camps. He commented that they fought *many* of them in his time spent in Camp Morton. He remembers one in particular and comments as such . . .

```
On top of a mountain in Wyalusing, PA I re-
member a big fire that they took us all to.
```

They took us there in trucks and we worked
all day long. When we got to a fire, the men
there would say, glad to have you here boys!
At this one, we stayed pert-near a week putting this one out. At some fires, we'd stay
all day and then go back to the camp that
night. At this particular fire, we stayed
there almost a week and slept on the ground.
We'd pull up next to a hot rock that was
heated by the fire and sleep next to it. It
kept us warm for the night. Just another way
we helped out the community . . . C. Libby

I further asked him about the methods of firefighting for the CCC boys and
he replied with a half-grin on his face . . .

We didn't have any fancy equipment up there
on top of the mountain, heck, they bare-
ly got us up there through the paths. All
we had were rakes, shovels and hand tools.
There were a few buckets to use if we were
near a stream at the time to throw some water on the hot spots. We used basic tools to
help smother the flames. If we didn't have
a tool in our hands we'd just pick up dirt
and throw it onto the hot spots and then
stomp it all the way out. We worked hard but
didn't think anything of it at the time. We
all wanted to help and we did! . . . C. Libby

After the days of the CCC Camps, the young Charles Libby found work in
his hometown on a bridge construction project. The Market Street Bridge
spans over the Susquehanna River which Charles was very familiar with due

to his love of swimming. Several young men were hired for the harder labor on this big project and Charles was anxious to be one of them.

> My brother Bob was the assistant foreman on the bridge project and told me to go and try to get the job. They knew I worked in the CCC Camp and knew that I would work hard for them, and I did! My job was to lay tracks along the side of the bridge for the street cars that used to run in our city. We used creosote-soaked railroad ties as a base and then the tracks were fastened to them. It took three of us at a time to move each rail tie. They were very heavy and it was hard work, but I was glad to have it at the time. I had to come home to help my father after the big flood from the CCC Camp and had no way of helping the family until I found that job . . . C. Libby

Hard work was something that Sgt. Libby was getting used to. By this age, he had done a wide variety of different jobs and enjoyed each of them. His ability to adapt from one job to the next and to handle the conditions were all a precursor to his next move which would be to join the 109th Infantry Unit of the US Army and eventually be a member of the 628th Tank Destroyer Battalion as an official command car driver which was no easy job in itself.

More Stories - From
The Command Car

$* \quad * \quad *$

IMAGINE IF YOU WILL, BEING fired upon randomly by an enemy sniper or at times non-stop by some of the bigger German guns with the noise so loud that you can not even hear yourself think. Further imagine, witnessing the new friend you just had lunch with getting shot in the head and dropping lifeless to the ground just inches away from you. Imagine if you will, collecting food rations to give to an ailing soldier within your unit and a German fighter pilot dropping down out of the clouds firing on either side of your feet as your unit watches in horror without any way of helping you. These events and many more occurred each and every day as the men of the 628th were in the thick of the fighting and most of the major European battles of the WWII. Sgt. Libby lived it and shares these vivid memories to have preserved within the history of what he and his fellow soldiers experienced.

Again, I feel compelled to mention that this follow up book should act as a book end of sorts in your reading and understanding of the life of Sgt. Charles Libby. Get yourself a copy of *From The Command Car* and it will help you in your understanding of these new stories from those days of WWII and use it to fill in the cracks that may appear while enjoying recall of the events he experienced and witnessed while serving our great country.

US MANEUVERS OF THE 628TH CONTINUED . . .

Before the young Libby or any of these soldiers knew what war was like, they had many months of training in the US to prepare themselves for what they may encounter. The time spent in these military training camps proved to be the key to their success while serving in the European Theater of Operations. Known as the *US Maneuvers*, soldiers found their specialties, learned how to master their future jobs and shared information with one-another in the event they were forced to perform a wounded or dead soldier's duties. These duties included reading maps, solving complex problems, building make-shift bridges, driving tanks, operating heavy machinery, fixing broken vehicles and learning how to fight with the weapons which were at their disposal. Soldiers all received intense training of the times to accomplish their ultimate goal of victory!

A STORY PULLED OUT OF *FROM THE COMMAND CAR* . . .

Three weeks of the required six recruits would normally spend near their hometown learning the special skills of the National Guard was all they had time for as the unit was ordered into regular federal service due to the increase of troop movement in Europe. At this point, the 109th Infantry Unit of The Pennsylvania National Guard became what Mr. Libby referred to as *regular army*. Quite a journey from a young boy jumping on trains, to the CCC Camps, to the Pennsylvania National Guard and now a member of The United States Army. Charles Libby's life in his younger years was full of excitement and plenty of personal satisfaction which laid down a solid foundation for years of experience for which was to follow.

Indiantown Gap, PA provided the men of this unit with a new home away from home. An encampment nestled in the mountains of Lebanon and Dauphin County, Fort Indiantown Gap is located twenty three miles northeast of Pennsylvania's capital city of Harrisburg. This would be the base of operations for these boys from the Williamsport unit. Between their rigorous schedule of maneuvers, which they were about to undertake to prepare for warfare on a completely different continent, to this point of intense training which would be of greater importance, it also started a period of time and countdown before shipping to Europe for the young men of this fresh new unit.

Combat training, concealment, camouflaging, map and compass reading, driving all military vehicles and basic machine and weapons operations would provide the troops with the necessary skill sets that they would need for their particular job as well as survival itself in the unfamiliar and rough terrain of the European continent. Preparedness and mock battles as a sort of *war games,* would be staged for various situations but still nothing could prepare them for the many horrors of combat that would befall them soon in their very young lives.

Preparedness was first and foremost for each branch of our military and prior to these young boys crossing an ocean that once only meant to them a place to vacation, these games and mock battles gave these new soldiers a look at different terrains to better prepare them for their possible locations within the European Theater of operations.

```
One of the first things we had to do was
to go into a building that they had set up
and walk its entire length without a gas
mask while they filled it with three differ-
ent kinds of smoke including small levels
of mustard gas. The barn-type of building
was really long and it took a while to get
through it. They made us walk and we weren't
allowed to run through it or we would have
to walk it again. It burned your eyes and
your throat really bad! Some of the guys in
my unit were throwing up afterward but we
all still had to do it at least one time.
```

```
They used gas in WWI and they knew that we
may have to deal with it like they did so
they wanted us to know what it was like.
None of us liked it at all! . . . C. Libby
```

The marksmanship award was achieved by shooting a series of five shots on the range which measured two-hundred yards. Several recruits lined up and had spotters who would verify the accuracy of your shots fired down range.

```
I qualified for this one without any prob-
lems. I paid attention and was very familiar
with guns from my hunting experience there
in the woods of Pennsylvania . . . C. Libby
```

Young Charles Libby had always taken pride in himself and the perception of how others saw him. He felt that if he was a soldier in the United States Army, he was going to look like a proud soldier. He took great care to always have his uniform pressed and required everything to be worn neatly and in its proper place. One particular memory of this time reflects that when company commander Captain Al Lentz called him forward in front of all the other soldiers and the newer recruits.

```
Captain Al Lentz said to me, Private Libby,
front and center. I walked up looking neat
and looking like a soldier. I was up there
all alone in front of the whole bunch and
beginning to feel a little uncomfortable.
Captain Lentz said to everyone, Now look at
this boy! He's only been here two weeks and
looks more like a soldier than all of you.
I expect you non-coms to look more like
this soldier here. I felt like melting at
that moment, but knew that I was acting and
```

looking like a good soldier which made me
very proud . . . C. Libby

One day while walking down the street in Fort Indiantown Gap, young Charles ran into his good friend Ernest Kirschbaum from Williamsport, who was now in the 109 Field Artillery. Not too happy with some of the guys in the unit at the time, Charles wondered if he could get out of his current unit and into the same one as his friend. He told Charles that on Sunday's you could go over to what they referred to as *Tent City* and sign up for the anti-tank outfit that they were just starting there. This would become the first field artillery combat unit for the United States Army. So, he did just that! He walked into Tent City on the very next Sunday and was anxiously greeted by the men there who asked him, "*Would you like to join us?*" They also asked him if he had any friends that he wanted to sign up as well. Charles signed up not only himself, but some of his friends that he knew wanted out of their current unit. Charles then went back to the camp and told one of the soldiers in particular that he was having the personal trouble with, that he was getting out of the unit. That same week, Sgt. Getchin came to the men while working on a map problem and announced, "*Libby, Bik, Phillips, Peterson*" and four other names which escape Sgt. Libby, "*You guys turn your bedding into the supply tent and report down to Tent City right away!*" So each of them followed the order and reported there happily. Mr.

Libby said that the unit was already established in their respective tents and assigned each of them to their own division of either A-Company, B-Company, C-Company or the Reconnaissance Unit.

We were all divided up and I was to immediately report to C-Company. I really didn't
care which unit they placed me in, I was
just glad to be out of my old outfit and
into this new one that was just forming.
The boys that I had signed up that day all

```
thanked me later on about signing them up.
I was a little worried that they would be
mad at me for doing it without them knowing,
but they all said that they were happier in
this new unit and out of the infantry. Now,
we were tank men! . . . C. Libby
```

A new addition to this previous story is that Marvin Phillips, one of the men that Charles had signed up to join the tank outfit, was due to be married the day they called all the new recruits to come to this newly forming tank unit.

```
Phillips came up to me and said, "What the
hell did you sign me up for? I'm getting mar-
ried tomorrow!" I looked at him, laughed and
told him that he'd have to make other plans.
He had to postpone his wedding ceremony and
join the new tank unit. About two years lat-
er, Phillips came up to me and said, "Thank
you Charlie for signing me up in this unit.
It didn't work out with that gal anyhow and
I'm happier here than in the infantry." I
told him, you're welcome and we both got a
good laugh out of it . . . C. Libby
```

At many of these military camps, simulated war games were conducted where soldiers and officers alike were put to the test in many areas of tactical combat. A *capture the flag* game, placed two different teams of men against one another to sharpen their skills and to find out their weaknesses *before* they were faced with actual combat. Drivers were not exempt from these games as they were in charge of transporting an officer to certain points and tactical locations to observe the battle that was taking place in an attempt to guide their team to victory. Sgt. Libby recalls the many war games that they designed for them and just how intense they became for these *wet behind the ears* soldiers, as well as how personal an officer would take it if his team was not the one to capture the opposing team's flag.

A red flag meant that you were on the side of the enemies Axis Forces and a blue flag meant that you were on the team of the United States and the Allied Forces. Each team had a goal of capturing the opposing team's men as well as the other team's flag as a final victory prize.

One such game recalled by Sgt. Libby, while on Tennessee maneuvers, placed him driving an umpire from the 44th division who was in charge of the games themselves. He was ranked a 1st Lieutenant and was supposed to be driven by another soldier. The driver asked Charles if he would switch with him, and out of kindness, he agreed to this more difficult task of driving the top officer and had no qualms about doing the favor for his fellow soldier.

Charles drove through the entire exercise and behaved much like he always did, paying attention to detail and performing like any soldier and driver should. The umpire was very impressed and thanked the young Libby for his good work that day. Charles went back to camp and thought nothing of it other than he had performed a good days work.

A day or so later, Sgt. Libby recalls that that same lieutenant returned to the camp looking specifically for him. He walked up to many in the camp asking, "*Where is the driver named Libby?*" Upon finding him, he shook his hand and asked if he could speak with him for a moment in private. Charles of course agreed and walked with the officer to a nearby office that was staged for a full-fledged colonel. As they entered the tent, they were both greeted by this high ranking officer. The 1st lieutenant had a seat and Charles was asked to stand at ease while the two officers began speaking about him and his exemplary performance during the past war games. The lieutenant spoke to the colonel as he kicked his feet up on the desk. He was very relaxed as he spoke and seemed to have a close relationship with this high ranking officer.

```
I was shocked to see him put both of his
feet up on the colonel's desk and how re-
laxed they both were talking about me. It
was just like talking to a couple of regular
GI's back in my own tent . . . C. Libby
```

It was the intent of this lieutenant to convince the colonel to bring the young Libby into their unit, but first he had to convince Charles that he would be appreciated and was needed. After asking him if he would like to come on over to their unit, Charles declined and said that he was comfortable in his tank unit and liked the job that he had been given. The lieutenant, not wanting to take no for an answer, asked the colonel directly, "*What can we make this soldier to come over to our outfit?*" Mr. Libby expressed to me that he could not believe what this officer had asked the colonel. The colonel responded back right away stating that they could promote him to either 1st Sgt. or to Sgt. Major. When Mr. Libby tells this story, his eyes get big, he smiles big and bright and usually tells me . . .

```
I was only a private at the time. I didn't
have that much schooling or education and
I knew that I could not perform up to the
level that they would have wanted me to. For
them to jump me up to that rank so quickly
would also not go so good with the other
fellas in the outfit and they would not re-
spect me like if I would had worked my way
up from the beginning in their unit . . .
C. Libby
```

So, with a sincere thank you and respectful salute to the two officers, Charles rejected the offer and returned back to his unit, not before the lieutenant reminding him of the great job he did for him and that his offer would stand anytime he was ready and willing to make the switch. And with a firm handshake and an appreciative thank you, Charles said, "*I have to get back to my outfit.*" Loyalty to his buddies as well as a missed opportunity for personal advancement adds another chapter in the development of this young man's military career and life's lessons.

When recalling this story, the one thing that he stresses is how important a proper education is for young people in the world. If he had been able to stay in school and if things would had been different, he would have had that promotion then and there and throughout the war could have moved up to a higher officers position. In his words of experience and wisdom, "*Education counts!*"

Maneuvers throughout the US were hard, long and also full of excitement for the young driver. But, they were not without a few minor setbacks along the way. One such setback occurred in a camp in Louisiana. A pool for the boys to cool off in after a long days training provided some comfort for this hard working tank outfit. Young men compete with one another regularly to prove themselves the better man in a variety of categories. This particular day found the unit competing in a diving contest. The young Charles was next on the board while others looked on. Now, Charles had been quite the diver back in his hometown of Williamsport, PA, diving off of the local bridges and rock formations near the Susquehanna River. His skill level was high and he was ready to do a little showing off for the other boys in his unit.

With a pool full of people, Charles approached his dive, only to be pushed off the board by his buddy Malvestuto. Charles, thinking quickly, saw that he was about to land in the water on top of a girl that was below him. Mid-air, he performed a half twist to avoid hitting her and hit the water very hard. During the twist, his foot came upward and hit his fingers, splitting them open at the webbing between two of them. After surfacing, Charles noticed that he was bleeding with the blood running down his arm from the now injured hand. Others noticed what had happened, including Malvestuto, and came to help him out of the pool, not knowing exactly what was the extent of his injury.

When they got me out, I felt my finger was
hanging down by my wrist. The webbing between the two of them on my left hand had
ripped open and there was blood running
everywhere! Malvestuto came to me and told
me that he was so sorry for doing that. He
said he never meant for that to happen. I
told him, all was okay and let's just forget about it. He was really sorry and really
shaken up over it . . . C. Libby

The quick acting Libby probably saved the life of the young girl that was below him just before hitting the water. He recalls this about the half twist he
instinctively he performed . . .

I did a half twist to throw my body in a
different direction so I wouldn't land in
her. If I had hit her, I know that I would
had broken her back or neck for sure! I was
glad that I was able to do what I did so I
didn't hurt her . . . C. Libby

Charles was taken to the hospital on base and received four stitches to repair
his fingers as well as having to keep the fingers taped together to support
them in the healing process. To this day, Mr. Libby can show you the faded
scars on his fingers where the injury happened. To him, they are a reminder
of the rough play that all the boys would give to each other during these hap-
pier times prior to their deployment to the bloody battlefields across Europe.

During this time, they were bivouacked near the camp until the weekend came around. This particular weekend, the local families from the community each sponsored a boy from the unit and received them into their
home for those two days. One such family had heard about Charles and made

a special trip to find him recovering from his injury. They asked him if he would like to come to their home and spend the weekend with them for some good old fashioned home comfort and food. Charles quickly accepted and went with them for a much needed break and a bit of family company.

```
They were really nice to me. The entire
community was always nice to all us boys!
They really seem to appreciate what we were
about to do for them by going to fight
the war. I had a nice bed to sleep in that
night and got fed really good food as well.
I talked to them about the CCC Camp and
shared other stories with them. I still
remember the nice chicken dinner they in-
vited me to and shared with me. They were
really nice people . . . C. Libby
```

One other story that haunts Sgt. Libby to this day, relates to an event that happened while on maneuvers in Livingston, LA. A disagreement between two young soldiers turned into a bloody scene and left one of the young soldiers dead.

Upon completing your first six weeks of basics, you were permitted to go to the local town's beer joint and have a few cold ones to celebrate your accomplishments and blow off some steam. Two rookies got into a heated argument and started to fist fight. The one soldier, with a glass in his hand, swung at the other, striking him in the side of the face and neck area. The glass shattered upon impact and cut the soldier's carotid artery. Sgt. Libby recalls the utter panic that quickly ensued.

```
I heard the two arguing and didn't think
too much about it. I was having a beer and
enjoying myself like all the other fellas.
```

Next thing I knew, I heard the glass breaking and pieces of broken glass hitting the
floor. I turned to see what had happened
and all I saw was blood squirting out of
that boy's neck and it was coming out really fast! I thought to myself right away,
that guy isn't gonna make it. The guy who
did it ran through the crowd of people
to try and hide himself but they ended
up finding him not too long after that.
Another soldier took his fingers and tried
to pinch off the artery to stop the blood,
but it just kept squirting out through his
fingers. Everybody got up and left and that
poor kid died right there in that bar. The
MP's came and took away the soldier that
did it and we never saw him again. Every
time I see a tulip-shaped glass, I think of
what I saw that day in Louisiana even before I went to war and saw even more death.
Poor kid . . . C. Libby

Another tale of times while taking a break from these grueling maneuvers,
took place while dancing with some girls that had come into town by the
truckloads to meet the local GI's in Camp Livingston, Louisiana. The young
and handsome Charles Libby was never too embarrassed to ask a girl for a
dance. Joe Walls, another GI that Charles knew from Headquarters, also
was fond of dancing and had his eye on one girl in particular.

Joe had danced with this one girl a couple of times and I saw her from across
the room. When they left the dance floor,
I made sure that I got to ask her for a

dance. We danced several times that night.
She was a pretty good dancer and was a
very pretty girl . . . C. Libby

Joe approached young Libby toward the end of the night when both of them
have had a few drinks in them. Joe Walls asked Charles why he was trying to
steal his girl. Charles being a little too intoxicated, told him that she wasn't
his girl and a fist fight ensued.

I was having a great time and probably had
a few too many beers that night. I didn't
think he would do it, but he punched me
right in the face. I flew back hard against
a tree and lay there on the ground trying
to catch my wits about me. My buddy Edward
Bik came over and punched Joe right in the
face and knocked him down off of the porch
and then came over to me and asked if I
was alright. He looked over at Joe and told
him to leave me alone and that he wouldn't
have been able to do that to me if I wasn't
drunk. Bik helped me up and the night of
fun was over . . . C. Libby

The story doesn't end there. I'd like to chalk one up for Sgt. Libby, to even
the score, and show how his Irish blood gets going when provoked by someone that is trying to harm others.

While in England, the GI's had their own little canteen where the boys
could get themselves a drink and unwind at night. Charles decided to go and
have himself a beer or two after his day's work was completed. A few of the
boys in his outfit were at the back of the canteen where they all saw Charlie.
He asked the boys what they were up to and they said to him that they were

trying to get a beer. He asked what they meant by trying and that's when the Irish really kicked in.

```
I asked the boys what they were doing and
they said that they were trying to get a
beer. I said to them, well, why don't you
just go get one. The boys told him that
they had tried, but Joe Walls had the bar
blocked and every time they would get to
the bar and try to order one, he'd block
it and bump against them and push them
away. They would get frustrated and walk
away not wanting to get into a fight. They
said that Joe was pretty drunk and that
he was probably looking for a fight . . .
C.. Libby
```

Charles approached the bar and saw Joe was clearly intoxicated. He said to him, "*Hi-ya Joe!*" and Joe turned around and said, "*Hey Libby!*" From there, Charles took control and began to remedy the situation for his thirsty friends of C-Company.

```
I said, Hey Joe, some of the boys back there
told me that you wouldn't let them up to
the bar to get a beer. He looked at me with
glazed eyes and said, no, I was just messing
around with them. They can come and get a
beer. I told him that I had heard it dif-
ferently and started to get mad remembering
how he sucker punched me over that girl in
Louisiana. I told him, Joe, you're like I
was that night you hit me and tonight, I'm
like you were, sober. I'm not gonna let you
```

```
do that to me again tonight, so you better
let these GI's get up here to the bar and
order themselves a beer. He looked at me and
said, you stole my girl that night. I raised
my voice and told him, they were there for
all of us, not just for you! He said, well,
I'm sorry Charlie, they can come up here
and get a drink. I told him, you're damn
right they can and if you get in their way
again I'm going to come over here and do
to you what you did to me. He said he was
sorry again and moved so that the others
could get their beer and enjoy the night.
He got my Irish up and I wasn't going to let
anything like what happened before happen
again . . . C. Libby
```

Now, the story doesn't end there. In a strange turn of events and a happy ending to all of the bitter feelings between these two soldiers, turn the clock ahead forty plus years to a reunion of these brave Tank Destroyers.

Charles looked forward to these reunions and this particular one was no exception. When he arrived and saw all of his friends he served with, Joe Walls was the first to approach him with an extended hand shake and greetings.

```
Joe was the first GI to come over to me
and say hello. He shook my hand and hugged
me and told me how happy he was to see me
and how sorry he was for what had hap-
pened so many years ago. He apologized many
times and wanted to make sure that we were
friends. I told him that I forgave him and
```

it was in the past. I was happy, he was
happy and throughout the night he told me
how nice of a guy I was and how sorry he
was that he had been like that. We became
great friends and all is well between myself and Joe Walls . . . C. Libby

PFC Joe Walls was awarded the Purple Heart for injuries suffered in battle during his time in the 628th Tank Destroyer Battalion, Headquarters
Company. Like so many of Sgt. Libby's 628th buddies, we are unaware if Joe
is still living or not at this time. We are currently researching the original
roster of men that shipped out within C-Company to see if Sgt. Libby has
the chance to a mini-reunion of sorts with any of his fellow company men.
To this day, my search sadly has not produced any.

Sgt. Libby standing, man #7 from left, 628th Reunion.
Photo circa 1986, photographer unknown.

Funny stories pop into the mind of Sgt. Libby about his past as I ask him questions or something I do that reminds him of a time long ago. One such story surfaced as we were talking about the German people themselves. Sgt. Libby had no hard feelings with the civilians he met there during the war. In fact, while still in the states during maneuvers, German families had immigrated here and were employed at some of the camps as cooks, laundry aids and all-around helpers.

In Camp Rucker, Alabama, Sgt. Libby remembers a German family that lived there near the base and were able to come in and make money by doing the men's laundry. The GI's there thought nothing of them being German except that they got out of Germany before the real mess started. Many did this and knew that they did not want to be a part of the new Germany or in other words, Hitler's Germany.

```
One day the grandmother of a young boy
brought him to our camp to see if some-
one there could help them with poison ivy
that the boy had gotten from the woods
nearby. His arm was covered in that stuff
and it looked terrible. He must have been
in a lot of pain. We really didn't know
what to do for him and she approached one
of the guys who was shaving. He looked at
her and said, hey put some of this shav-
ing cream on it and it will heal right up.
We all kind of chuckled because we didn't
know whether it would work or not. We were
kind of busy and just passed the buck to
him for the solution. Well, after putting
the Omega Shaving Cream on the infected
area, a week later she brought him back to
```

```
show us and thank us for the tip that had
healed it up! We couldn't believe it did
the job. I still laugh and think back to
that time but I remember that I was glad
that it helped the little German boy get
well . . . C. Libby
```

I always find it interesting as a civilian, that soldiers get to qualify with weapons and use them on the battlefields that I see in movies or documentaries, played with army men that carried them and that I will never get the opportunity to fire or handle. One such weapon is the *hand grenade*. I asked Sgt. Libby about his experience with this fascinating weapon of destruction and he commented this . . .

```
You had too throw it from a pit that you
climbed down into. They showed us how to
pull the pin, how to throw it and then you
had to get down! Shrapnel would be fly-
ing when it blew up, so you had to protect
yourself. On the vehicle, it was the job of
the gunner to throw them if they needed to.
I only threw one during my time in battle.
A German soldier stood in the middle of the
road firing on us one time and after he
got scared or ran out of bullets, he turned
and ran. He ducked down into a doorway and
I saw where he went. I reached behind the
seat and grabbed a hand grenade and when
I pulled up next to that doorway, I pulled
the pin and tossed it down there. Besides
the Germans laying in the road, half dead
that I was ordered to keep driving and ran
over with the vehicle, this was the only
```

time that I had to kill a German soldier in battle. I had to do it, he was just shooting right at me and was trying to kill me and probably would have started shooting at me again if I hadn't done it . . . C. Libby

Another weapon that he mentions within his first book with the enemy firing it, but does not mention himself is the *bazooka*. When asking him about his experiences with this unique weapon, he comments as such . . .

The bazooka was like a big piece of stove pipe. You had to really hold it tight and lean into it when you shot. You also had to put one foot forward so it would not kick you too hard from the pressure. You would adjust the angle of it up or down to shoot closer or to shoot a little further away. An Italian guy in our unit was taking his first shot with one and didn't lean into it and ended up going ass backwards. He did a complete somersault in the air. We called guys like that yard birds. Guys that didn't have all their marbles upstairs and didn't listen to instructions very well. Everybody was laughing after it happened. The infantry guys really were the ones that shot them anyhow. We didn't have one on my vehicle . . . C. Libby

The M20 Scout Command Car, which Sgt. Libby drove, had a 50 caliber gun mounted on a turret that moved 360 degrees. I asked Sgt. Libby about other weapons that may have been on this vehicle and he responded with a big list for me.

I had a Thompson sub-machine gun with
clips, a carbine rifle with extra belts of
ammo, plenty of rounds for the 50 caliber, we all carried pistols and knives and
there were two different kinds of grenades
on board . . . C. Libby

I was curious in my interviews whether or not Sgt. Libby had to dig fox holes
while serving in the European Theater and he responded very quickly to this
question as such . . .

I only ever had to dig one fox hole and
that was in Indiantown Gap, PA before I
went to war while on maneuvers. That one
fox hole was enough! I'd seen many of them
in the war. British troops sitting in one
drinking tea at 10, 2 and 4 o'clock, old
ones left over from WWI, new ones dug by
our infantry units, but I was fortunate
enough that I drove the command car and
wasn't required to dig any fox holes. One
time a buddy of mine had a Polish soldier
that was fighting with the Germans dig one
for him so he didn't have to do it. He told
him to dig fast because he was digging
his own grave. He slowed way down after he
heard that. Turned out, he was digging the
hole so that we could bury all of our gar-
bage to hide it from the German soldiers
and prevent them from getting any extra
information on how many of us there were
in the area . . . C. Libby

MORE FROM THE THEATER OF OPERATIONS IN EUROPE . . .

So many stories for Sgt. Libby at 100 years old run together as to just where he was at the time. In my many interviews, I thought that the substance of the story was more important than the location unless it had to do with a specific documented battle. When it came to that, it was easy for him to remember just where he was. It was all the other *side-stories* that sometimes made him sit back and really think for a minute or two as to where he actually was.

There are also some stories that did not have much bearing on his experiences, just a glimpse of the past that he remembered as we gabbed about his time spent there. Some of them about the many women he had chasing him and the ones he chased himself during those times. Keep in mind, he was a good looking American GI that looked much like a famous movie star, Australian-born actor Errol Flynn. There were several of those memories and one such story brings a half grin to his face as he tells of a romantic encounter he had while in Heiligenstadt, Germany where this tale of boy meets girl takes place.

Bik, Sill, Peterson and Libby are all on a much needed break leaning up against his command car in town. Down the road strolls a beautiful girl with her mother toward the men. What the guys sitting with the young Libby didn't know was that he had already met her, her parents and started a little romance with her prior to that day. He played it cool with the guys as they all remarked about her beauty and how they were going to try to talk to her and start one of their own.

```
I just sat there and waited until she got
closer and listened to these guys talking
about her. She got close to our vehicle and
she looked at me and said, "Charlie, we go
now?" My buddies eyes almost popped out of
```

```
their heads when they heard her talking to
me . . . C. Libby
```

Charles had been using his down time in the area by shooting crows in an old barn for a local farmer. This farmer, her father, did not like American soldiers but for some reason took a liking to young Libby.

```
She was a young girl and very pretty. I think
her name was Tiga Louie. She thought I was
very handsome and could speak some broken
English that she had learned at school. I
was always respectful to her and I think
that is why her father liked me. After we
pulled out of that area, I never saw her
again. I hope that she was alright during
the rest of the war . . . C. Libby
```

I try my best to spark memories and to pull things out of the mind of this 100 year old veteran and choose many things that I feel would not only be interesting to others, also things that I find to be essential facts that readers would appreciate about a command car driver and his responsibility of keeping an officer safe.

Officers can be seen by enemy snipers, foot soldiers, tanks, enemy planes and are a prize to their unit. To kill or capture an officer was a great victory to a German soldier and potentially a great source of information for their entire unit which could have been a tipping point in the entire war.

```
I knew I was in charge of keeping my of-
ficer safe as the driver. I had to keep my
eyes open at all times in all directions
while driving. Sometimes it was harder when
```

it was dark. I had to run the cat eyes, blue
lights we used at night on our vehicles that
were very dim but magnified to see or even
just use the moonlight to navigate. During
the daytime, my gunner and I watched in
every direction to keep him safe. It was
my number one responsibility and I took it
seriously! . . . C. Libby

According to Sgt. Libby, there were about twelve M-20 Command Cars
within his unit. These specialized vehicles, all operated by skilled drivers, had a top speed of about 35-40 miles per hour. They were rugged
and needed to be for what they were asked to do day in and day out. He
also remembers that it was his job to make sure it operated properly and
it was full of gasoline at all times. The moment they stopped to check
everything, a truck would supply him with the precious fuel to fill the
35 gallon tank it had. Keeping a watch on the gas gauge and all other
aspects of the vehicle was just one of the many responsibilities for a
driver.

I was the lead vehicle for C-Company. Captain
Jones thought that I was a pretty good driver and that made me very proud. I remember
one night that we had to drive in complete
darkness due to being in enemy held territory. I looked back at him and said, I hope
there's no ditch. He asked me if I could see
the road and I told him that I was using the
moonlight to help me and was staying close
to the edge to stay on the road and not
to hit any land mines in the middle. After
driving for quite a while, you would know
the vehicle and what she could do and if you

got too close to the edge of the road, you'd
start to feel your vehicle not grabbing like
it should and you would have to adjust it.
If you saw a lump in the road ahead of you,
you'd try to shoot it or throw rocks to hit
it because it was probably a mine that the
Germans placed there. Also, when you were
traveling down a road and the convoy of infantry men saw something, they'd throw their
hands up for us to stop and we'd do the same
and it would go down the line so everyone
knew to pay extra attention and to stop where
they were so they could examine the situation. Sometimes we'd have to stop because
of the piano wire they would string across
the road to try and cut our heads off. You
couldn't see it until you were right up to
it. That was scary stuff! They would check
for about 5-10 miles when they found these
things and clear it, then we could continue
down the road we were on . . . C. Libby

The dangers that every soldier had around them at all times was great.
The tasks that a lead vehicle driving an officer was even greater! A command car driver is the *unsung hero* of WWII. He made split second decisions, he drove in a wide variety of conditions, he kept the vehicle
from blowing up from German boobie-traps, he made sure that it ran
properly, he ensured the safety of all people on board including an officer that was in charge of many others around him and he also made sure
that they were in the right place at all times thanks to his understanding
of complex map reading which he was trained in back in the US during
their maneuvers.

I further asked Sgt. Libby what the policy was if captured by the enemy. I thought that I should dismiss the black and white war movie protocol of name, rank and serial number to empty my cup of sorts and get the truth from an actual WWII soldier. Well, I guess I should have stayed with that old formula. He told me exactly that! He was to give his name, rank and serial number, with one addition.

```
We were supposed to tell them the complete
opposite of the truth! No directions, no
troop locations and try to throw them off
their game . . . C. Libby
```

Sgt. Libby does not remember any of the men within his company ever getting captured. With that said, not many that were even *KIA*, killed in action. The unit sustained very few deaths and major injuries. The infantry men that traveled with the tank unit sustained more casualties due to the different boobie-traps that they were more susceptible to being on the ground and doing what they had to do in the actual close combat.

```
We never underestimated the enemy! They
wanted to win just like we did. They were
brainwashed by Hitler and they didn't care
what they had to do to get us . . . C. Libby
```

Sgt. Libby does make mention of a guy he bonded with while at Fort Indiantown Gap, PA prior to shipping over to Europe from his unit that was killed in action. Sgt. Jim Luvender, another PA native, was KIA while bravely fighting the Germans that were attacking his platoon. Sgt. Libby explains what he had heard about his close friend's death from other GI's . . .

```
He was just like Audie Murphy. He made his
way up on to the back of a tank that was
```

disabled and got behind the 50 caliber gun
and started mowing down the Germans during
The Battle of The Hurtgen Forest. He did that
for quite a while all by himself and then
an artillery shell hit right by the tank and
a piece of shrapnel tore into his body and
killed him. He was a good guy and we were
pretty good friends. I still miss him very
much and think of him often . . . C. Libby

Sgt. Libby standing with close friend Sgt. Jim Luvender.
Photo circa 1944, photographer unknown.

Enemy planes seem to be something that caused more trouble for
the unit than anything. Having to pull off the main roads, camouflaging
their vehicles, taking cover in a ditch, infantry digging fox holes when on

down-time, all were due to the low flying enemy planes that the Germans would employ regularly.

```
Sometimes they flew so low and so slow that
you could almost walk as fast as they were
flying. They were only looking to stir some-
thing up with us. They wanted to find us by
drawing our fire and then they could pin-
point us and start shooting and shelling us
with their big guns. They were smart, but so
were we! . . . C. Libby
```

HERE IS A STORY PULLED OUT OF *FROM THE COMMAND CAR* ON THESE GERMAN FIGHTER PLANES.

The men of the 628th didn't have much time at all to relax during their time spent in the area of the Hurtgen Forest or anywhere else for that matter. Sgt. Libby recalls that when the B-Company needed a break, they moved in and when A-Company needed a rest, they moved in as well. They kept the rotation going and C-Company never got a long break to recover, they just kept moving and taking care of business day after day.

This proved to be one of the toughest battles they faced during the entire war. A brief break in the shooting at night would be a strategic move on the part of both sides to keep locations of troops hidden and prevent attacks in the darkness, but the unit was at the ready the entire time between the shelling exchanges.

```
I remember parking my vehicle under an ap-
ple tree one night as I stood on guard duty.
A German plane would always fly over to try
and draw enemy fire from us. We were told to
never fire at him! We called him Bed-check
```

Charlie. He was so close that I could read the numbers on the wing of his plane. He moved very slowly and I could not believe that his engine didn't stall out. He would fire some rounds down in several directions trying to get us to fire at him so that they could accurately lay artillery fire on us. I sat on guard behind the 50 caliber gun just wishing that I could shoot him down. I could have easily gotten him but was told never to fire at him because it would give away our unit position. I'd mumble to myself, you bastard, I could shoot you out of the sky right now! It was so frustrating to me and I always said, there is not enough time to get scared and if you did get scared, you'd flip your lid! . . . C. Libby

**Sgt. Libby reenacting his position on the 50 cal. gun
at the 2017 Lewisburg Veterans Parade.**
Photo 2017, photographer Steve Hunter.

ANOTHER GREAT STORY OF GERMAN PILOTS TRYING THEIR BEST TO GET THE COMMAND CAR DRIVER . . .

Leaving the area of the Hurtgen Forest led the men into a valley which was populated with small homes in a small village setting. Shortly after staging the unit near some farmhouses, Charles needed to go to the rear echelon to get more 10-in-1 rations for his command car. During this short walk toward the supply truck, Charles heard the roar of a German fighter plane nearing this small village. As the German fighter plane geared up to make it over the top of a tree, Charles noticed the plane zeroing in on a fuel truck which was near him. Charles kept walking to where he was going, but now at a faster pace and heard the noises that would prove to be one of the closest calls to being shot and killed that he would receive throughout the entire war!

```
The good Lord Jesus Christ was watching
over me that day. I never got excited, it
happened so quickly! I didn't even run, I
just kept on walking. The plane started
strafing the ground to try and hit the fuel
truck in front of me that was loaded with
five gallon cans of gasoline. Bullets were
hitting the ground on both sides of me. If
he had banked to the left or to the right,
I would have been hit for sure! He only
made one run by me and pulled up over some
trees and then he disappeared. There must
have been at least twenty rounds fired at
me on both sides of my body. When I looked
back, I could see the fire coming out of
his wings. He knew he only had one chance
to get it and knew that we had all kinds
```

```
of guns sitting there that would get him on
his next pass . . . C. Libby
```

As Charles returned to his command car, back at the front of the staging area, several of the soldiers in his company who saw the incident continued to ask him if he was alright and if he was hit. Many commented that they thought he had gotten hit by the bullets and couldn't believe that he was still alive. They joked about the near-fatal experience but were glad that one of their own was safe and had made it through that close call unscathed. The men continued to joke with him as he walked back to his command car with the much needed 10-in-1 rations in hand.

```
It was a close call! I was glad that he was
trying to hit the fuel truck and not me!
This kind of thing was starting to happen
so often that I did not realize how danger-
ous this could have been. You get used to
the shots and all of the noises when you've
been around it for a while . . . C. Libby
```

Zygmund Dyda was a colorful character from the unit that Sgt. Libby refers to quite often. His dangerous antics while serving made for many stories within our first book. Snipping the wire to free a booby trap within a doorway, climbing into a German fighter plane to retrieve a German pistol just before the plane blew up and burst into flames and countless other stories that Sgt. Libby shared with me throughout our conversations. We thought it fitting to honor him with a photo in this newest book.

Although Dyda did all of those crazy things, he was a good man and became great friends with Sgt. Libby and fought the entire war with bravery and loyalty to his fellow Tank Destroyer Battalion mates.

Dyda pictured with local German girl as he and other GI's take advantage of their celebrity status with the locals. *Photo WWII, photographer unknown.*

In my research of soldiers of C-Company, I look at the photos and notice that there were no black soldiers within his unit. It struck me as being strange and I asked him about this particular subject.

There were no blacks in my unit. Back then, we all called them colored people. That's just how it was. There were some of them that cooked for units and I heard of some in other outfits that were only blacks, but none were in mine. They were all nice fellas and I never understood why they didn't let them into the tank units, but I guess those were the times and the army had their own

```
set of rules then. I liked them and didn't
much care for the way they were all treated
there and back in the states . . . C. Libby
```

Sgt. Libby does comment on the state of the armed services at present time and showed much frustration in the fact that transgender soldiers were permitted to wear the uniform of a United States soldier. To him, it is a ridiculous display of a changing army and it caters to the sick and perverted mental illness of men that is a distraction to the others as well as one purpose of the army, to make boys into *men*! He was very happy to hear that President Trump had reversed this rule of allowing them to enter and have their identity treatments paid for by the US Government.

Also, after being in war and seeing the pressure, the horror, the blood and the extreme physical demands that it places on a person, he does not think that it is wise for females to have been deployed to the front lines. He also thinks that separating them from the men would eliminate many problems and keep the men more focused on the job at hand, which is war and fighting it without any distraction.

After talking to him about many of the incredible weapons they had in WWII, the subject of the German boobie-traps and foot mines came into his mind and he shared an additional tidbit that he didn't share with me in my first book on this interesting topic.

```
We used to carry a small piece of slate rock
in our ruck sacks in case we stepped on a foot
mine. You would stand very still and take the
slate and slide it under your foot to keep
pressure on the mine so that you could get
your foot off of it. If you stepped off, the
pressure would release and the mine would go
off and blow your foot, your leg and other
```

parts off of your body. I saw it happen to
guys and it was awful. We were pretty careful
when it came to their traps they set for us.
I never stepped on one and I am glad that I
didn't have to deal with any of that like the
infantry did. Also, I never ran over a mine
in my vehicle. Many times I saw something
wrong with the road ahead and would stop for
the infantry to check it out and most of the
time, I was right! . . . C. Libby

The men of the 628th were always in the middle of hot battles and during any
type of search of homes that were unoccupied or inhabitable, Charles would
look for food to bring aboard his vehicle to feed himself and the others that
he transported. Always leaving some behind for others, he would make sure
as not to be greedy and only take what he knew he and his men would be
able to use.

A routine stop with heavy fighting nearby led Charles into a home that
produced some food including potatoes and some bottles of cognac. As he
made his way past an old railroad bridge, he could here Germans speaking in
the culvert below the bridge. He further examined this potentially harmful
situation to find that it was German citizens rather than enemy combatants
trying to flee the heavy fighting between the Americans and the Nazis.

I saw that there were some young girls, a
few adult women and a few men below the
bridge. They looked to be very scared as
well as hungry. In my broken German that I
had learned, I asked them what was going on.
They replied that they were waiting for the
heavy fighting to stop and then they would
move on. They were scared of me at first.

They looked very hungry and I asked them if
they had eaten recently. They told me that
they had not in some time. I moved toward
them and assured them that I was not going
to shoot and offered them the food that I
was carrying for myself and for the men on
my vehicle. I took them to the cellar of
the home that I had found these items and
told them that they would find some more in
there. The door was locked and they motioned
that they would not be able to get into the
cellar because it was locked. I drew my
pistol and shot the lock off and told them
that they would be able to get into there
now! They were very happy that I didn't try
to harm them and that I was helping them to
get the much needed food. I returned to the
inside of the house and gathered up some
more things for myself once again and as I
made my way back to the command car. They
all thanked me in German many times over
and over again. I waived and said you're
welcome and moved back to the business I
needed to be doing at my car . . . C. Libby

This is just one more of the many ways that Sgt. Libby demonstrated his ability to distinguish between the enemy and the people that were truly trapped in a society where an evil-doer ruled with an iron fist. This was truly a time of confusion and unrest as well as blood being spilled around every corner.

The German people were wonderful! They were
told to salute or be shot! They didn't all
follow Hitler, but what could they do? It

was up to us soldiers to help those people
that just wanted to get away and live their
lives. I hoped that all of those people I
helped got to safety after the fighting was
over . . . C. Libby

The Staff Sgt. named Leo, became a very good friend of Charles during his
time in the US Army. *Fat Boy* was the name that he was tagged with by the
men due to his bigger size. Sgt. Libby always recalls him with a big smile on
his face and enjoys sharing stories about this special guy.

We were over in England and the Germans
conducted raids at night and they lasted
forever it seemed. We were at a British base
and it was equipped with a bomb shelter that
we would all go down into when they started
to bomb the area around the base. I have to
hand it to the British, when a German plane
would fly over and they got one light up on
them, in a matter of seconds there would be
a dozen lights on them and then you would
see the tracers of the flak hitting the
plane. If they got a light on them, they
were surely a goner! Anyhow, one morning
Fat Boy came out into the base yard area
and had a skinned up head, red nose and his
chin was all torn up as well. He was walking like a soldier marching and counting
out loud. I said, hey Fat Boy, what are you
doing? He looked at me and said that tonight
he would know just how many steps it was
from his bunk to the bomb shelter. I asked
him, why? He said that last night when they

shut down all the lights and he was running
to get there, he ran right into a metal pole
and it knocked him on his ass! I laughed so
hard and he just smiled and kept pacing off
the number of steps it would take him to get
there safely on the next round of German
fighters trying to get us . . . C. Libby

Sgt. Libby and Fat Boy posing after some boxing practice.
Photo circa 1944, photographer unknown.

From the file of *"what the heck?"* . . . Have you ever watched a war movie
and wondered when they urinated or made a bowel movement? I did! So I
asked him point blank, *"When did you pee?"*

How did you poop in the middle of a battle?" Well, knowing this man, I knew
that I would get an answer that would either satisfy my curiosity or come
with a smart remark.

When we stopped anywhere, you made good
time of that and did your thing. You stayed
close to your vehicle and you got it done
fast! I never had a problem with that and
controlled my bodily functions pretty good.
I never went in my pants or had to fall behind the others to do my thing. I'd see guys
from the infantry step off the road from
time-to-time and take a leak, but they were
always careful about landmines and boobie
traps set by the Germans. So, they stayed
close to the road or path we were on at the
time. Well, I guess I did alright in that
department while I was there. I'm not sure
about some of the others, but I never seemed
to have a problem with it . . . C. Libby

I asked him about hygiene and trying to keep to the strict military code of
being clean shaven and clothing being satisfactory to a commanding officer.
This question was brought up after I met another WWII soldier that told me
a story about being chewed out by General Patton himself while sitting in
a fox hole and having a scruffy face known as a twelve o'clock shadow. He
responded as to this question as such . . .

I never really had a problem with my beard
growing too fast so that helped me. When we
would stop for a refueling or to get ammu-
nition from the trucks that would come up
from the rear echelon, we would fill our
helmets with a little water and lather up
fast to give ourselves a quick shave. I never saw anyone get into any trouble from not
being shaved, but we were C-Company and we

were always in the battles with very little
time to think about shaving. Our clothes
were a very different story. We tried to
make sure that we rinsed them out at any
stop, like a house we were checking or the
fountain we bathed in when we liberated
Paris. It would get pretty bad at times, the
smell, that you could not stand yourself.
So, when we could, we would either change
into some fresh clothes if we had them with
us in our ruck sack or try to quickly wash
them by hand . . . C. Libby

A cup of Joe or java. I had always heard that term used for coffee and wondered if this was something that the men really appreciated on those long
roads and cold mornings. That hot, black cup of liquid beans that wakes you
up and gives you that extra pep in your step. I wondered if this simple little
pleasure that we may take for granted held a special place in the hearts of the
men while they were in a battle-ridden area that would provide them with
that one simple comfort of home.

We had instant coffee that was like a pow-
der that we'd mix up to have a cup of
java. I wasn't much of a coffee drinker
but liked and still like hot cocoa. Other
guys liked coffee and drank it often. The
British liked their tea and we saw them
drink that often! I didn't carry coffee in
my supplies on the M-20 because my officer
didn't really care for it either. But the
cocoa on those cold mornings was a really
nice treat. I still like my cocoa with a

meal. I guess it goes back to my days on
the dynamite crew in the CCC Camp. I always
drank it there . . . C. Libby

I personally wanted to know more about the men that rode in Sgt. Libby's
vehicle during the war. I asked him to describe them and tell me a little bit
more so I could share with you as well, the readers. I think that having a better understanding of the person would aid in reading the stories and help to
develop a character-type of image within your mind as you read.

Edward Bik, my gunner and one of my very
best friends. Bik was Polish and was a pretty big guy. He was very nice and always
kept his cool in battle. He was a believer
in God and was one of the boys that cop-
ied the Letter of Protection which he carried in his pocket through the entire war.
He really was a close buddy and we watched
out for one another quite a bit! He wanted
to learn how to dance and asked me to help
him, so I did. He would go to all the dances
with me and watched how I moved with the
ladies. He started to pick it up pretty good
after a while. When he was on that 50 caliber gun, he was pretty good. I remember him
hitting German planes and the smoke coming
out of the back as they flew away to try
and get back to their territory to land. I
used to see him at the reunions long ago
but haven't seen him since. I do miss him
and will always consider him to be a great
friend . . . C.. Libby

Joseph Malvestuto and Edward Bik. *Photo circa 1944, photographer unknown.*

Peterson, the radio man and another great friend, had the crucial job of getting transmissions and sending them alike to HQ during the war. Charles and Petersen also became close friends and stayed close to one another during their time in the war. I find it semi-humorous that Sgt. Libby refers to him as Pete Peterman when his name is actually Robert Peterson.

```
Peterman was a quiet fella. He was really
smart and did a great job with the duties of
the radio and all the orders that came from
HQ. He would also come with us to the dances
and would enjoy himself. We didn't get as
close as Bik and I did, but we were great
```

friends all through the war. He was the one
that got the message about those four truck
loads of our boys that we saved. He also was
with me when I took those six German prisoners on the dike. We saw a lot of things
together and I miss him just like I miss Bik
and my other buddy Sill . . . C. Libby

Robert "Pete Peterman" Peterson. *Photo circa 1945, photographer unknown.*

Robert Sill was another great friend that Sgt. Libby refers to often in
his stories. Especially the time that he pressed a pistol into his hand and
thought it wouldn't go off if he kept it firm against the barrel, as told in
our first book. That event led to another humorous story that I enjoy Sgt.
Libby telling.

```
I saw Sill at the reunion in West Middlesex
and I asked him how his hand was doing. He
was there with his wife at the time and told
me that it was fine. He showed me that there
was only a small mark but he did not regret
doing it. I asked him why and he told me
that he had met his wife from that accident.
She was his nurse! We all laughed and I told
him that I was glad that it all worked out
for the both of them. I miss Sill and all my
other buddies from the war, but time goes by
and life goes on . . . C. Libby
```

There are stories about other soldiers doing great things and some doing things that really are not for everyone's ears to hear. This particular story that we opted not to put into the first book. After careful consideration of what we know about the mental stress soldiers go through during war and wanting to get any story out there about what Sgt. Libby saw while serving, I have decided to write about it now. It is a sad story in many ways about the behavior of some of the soldiers that we sent over there to fight a bloody war half way across the world without understanding just what they may be *turned into* with the stress of war and how their nerves and overall decision making in many stressful situations may change.

It was a little fuzzy on the location, but he believes that it occurred in the town of Mannheim, Germany. The details are still very distinct within his mind though . . . Charles and a few other soldiers from his unit were walking through a street which intersected a narrow alley very near a business with fancy windows where people could see into the street below. In the alley, but very near to this main street, there were two US Marines with two very young local girls. Their intent was to have sexual relations with them right there in that alley in plain view of all the local residents. Sgt. Libby remarked that this was an unacceptable behavior of anyone that wore the United States uniform. One of the other men from the unit that saw what was about to occur remarked to the two men that maybe they should take them back deeper into the alley so that they would not be seen by anyone and stir up any trouble with the locals. Sgt. Libby further explains,

> They didn't like that one of our guys was telling them what to do and wanted us to mind our own business. They were very cocky and thought that since they were Marines, they were better than a GI. They came out of the alley toward us in their dress uniforms fixing themselves and zipping up their uniform pants as they came closer. They looked at us with a pissed off, conceited look and told us to mind our own damn business and further spouted off that they would be home soon and just maybe, they would be doing the same thing to our mothers, sisters or our wives before we even got home. That didn't sit too well with one of our guys who just came off of the front lines. As they were starting to laugh at what they had just said to all of us, the unknown GI pulled out his pistol, firing two shots and hit each of them right in the stomach. They both dropped to the ground right in their tracks and lay there dead in that alley. I can't remember who it was that did it and didn't know the guy that was in this small group I was walking with at the time, but I could not believe my eyes when it happened.

He was so mad and it happened so fast that
none of us could have done anything to stop
him . . . C. Libby

Shortly after the two were shot, the men walked out of the alley, passing two
MP's that were walking to the scene of the shots that they both heard. There
were other soldiers and people around making it a little hectic at that time
as the MP's started asking everyone, *"What happened, did you see anything?"*
Sgt. Libby indicated that the boys all said, what, *"What are you talking about?"*
as they just kept on moving away from the scene as the two MP's started to
access the situation.

We got out of there real fast! Nobody said a
thing and nobody talked about it again until I told you now. There was nothing that
I could do and we were moving out that same
day to get back to the fighting. It was a
horrible thing that happened, but those guys
seemed as if they were about to start a fight
with us as well. They both had pistols on
their hips and were real mad that we stopped
them from having sex with those two young
girls. I put it out of my mind and did not
remember it until we sat down to start the
book. Remember, I was a young soldier and
had heard about that stuff happening but
had never seen it. I never saw that guy that
did it again and after seeing all that I had
seen so far in the bloody war, it was just
another day to all of us of who were fighting
and sorting out the bad guys, even if some
of them were our own soldiers . . . C. Libby

As Sgt. Libby told me this story, several emotions came across in the tone of his voice, sadness, anger, disbelief, as well as showing all these deep emotions on his face. The mental scars that soldiers carry with them don't fade like some that you can see on the outside of their body. These scars haunt them through the night and come up in conversations when a memory is stirred up just like this one that he has lived with for over seventy years. Not the best of events that he remembers, but history of the untold horrors and misfortunes of war that would have gone untold until now.

Before shipping home to the states, several weeks behind the rest of his unit, Charles was in Germany along with a lieutenant who was having his picture painted by a German artist. According to Sgt. Libby, the artist noticed the Errol Flynn look alike and asked if he could paint his picture as well. Sgt. Libby elaborated to me the details of this last memory of his time over there in Europe . . .

```
I was there with this lieutenant and the
German artist noticed me and asked the of-
ficer if he could also paint me. He re-
ally wanted to do it but time was short
so he used water-colors to speed it up. He
asked me to come back again and he would
do it in oils but I was shipping out and
I wasn't going to miss my only chance to
get home because of a painting. I like it
and wished I could have gone back again to
him after the war for the other one. I of-
fered him money but he wouldn't take any.
I guess they appreciated us so much being
over there that it was important for him to
do it for me . . . C. Libby
```

A young Sgt. Charles Libby done in water colors by unknown German artist.
Photo 2017 by Steve Hunter.

Approximately fourteen years after Sgt. Libby left the US Army, he joined back up with men from his National Guard Unit and performed with their drill team in parades and other military functions. The Muncy Flying Eagle Color Guard *"Roost of The Eagles"* used various cadences used by the military when marching in basic training were placed to music that the bands either in front or in back of them would play. White wooden rifles held in their hands, donning black uniforms and white helmets, the men of the 109th and others from the area, would show the crowds their routines they all worked so hard on in their spare time as a tribute to their service days.

```
We would practice in Muncy, PA in a large
field or in a big garage that someone would
allow us to use. We'd meet before the event
and work on our routines and then would
march for the crowds at the local parades.
Sometimes we'd travel a little farther and
twice won second prize for our performance.
```

```
I really liked it but after a few years of
doing it, it dissolved . . . C. Libby
```

Sgt. Libby's son Chuck also commented on how sharp the men looked and how he, as a child, went to many of their events and remembers how good they all looked as they did their routines. Still a proud memory of both the Libby men. Also to be noted, this group won the VFW State Championships in the following years : 1961, 1968, 1974 and 1975.

Over there, over there, spread the word, spread the word, over there. That the yanks are comin', the yanks are comin'! And we won't stop comin' til we're over, over there!

The words to a popular song that was played during that time of WWII. The Americans were coming and they meant business! They weren't going to stop coming until the job was finished and were convinced that they would be the victors of this long and bloody war. The true grit spirit of the American worker back home, the patriotic conviction of the soldiers going over there and the fact that God himself was on their side says it all.

```
We all had an important job to do and we did
it well . . . C. Libby
```

They all knew that if they didn't do this job that everything we knew as a country and had worked so hard for up til then would had disappeared at the hands of a lunatic with the last name of Hitler. But thanks to men with the last names of Libby, Bik, Peterson, Luvender, Malvestuto, Luckey, Gallagher, D'iorio, Kratz, Dyda, Deffenbaugh, Donald, Brooking, Missigman, Yonkovig, Hunter, Leo, Erdos, Knopf, Scanlon, Phillips and the many thousands more from every background and walk of life, put their lives on hold and went "*over there*" to get the job done. God bless you all and many of us still want to thank you to this day for your great sacrifices.

Souvenirs and Memories

∗ ∗ ∗

WE ALL IN SOME FORM or fashion collect items that make us happy, feed our personal interests or for purposes of triggering memories of a time gone by that we wish to remember. From baseball cards to coins to photos to vintage toys, when we hold or look at them they take us back to a place and time we remember. Some of these thoughts are happy ones and some may be sad to us. But, they all do one thing, they remind us of who we are, what we have done and where we have been.

Soldiers are no different than any of us with the exception of the what they have done and just where they have been. WWII and the European Theater of Operations for Charles Libby and the other men of his unit, was a treasure-trove of souvenirs, trinkets and other items that would trigger memories of the war far into their future. Rules were put in place as to what they could bring back personally or ship home, how much they could accumulate and whether or not it was completely illegal to possess certain items. But, even with that said, many of the men managed to bring home items that in a sense were saved to be shared with all of us as a part of history all these years later!

At our work station, his kitchen table, while tracking the movement of his unit, it was filled with maps, his field glasses, photo albums, loose war pictures, his German pistol and assorted documents of his service records.

At times, our work station would stay like this for multiple days and would get even fuller as we added topics, preventing his family from a meal at their own dining room table. Everyone was pleased when we finally finished a section and items could be placed back into a safe place.

Thank God they brought many of these items home so that we can examine, learn from and chronicle them. Many items regretfully were destroyed either in battles or during the occupation period by our troops as a type of *in your face* to the now defeated German and Japanese soldiers. To be able to have the privilege to place your hands on some of these items or view them within a museum gives us the ability to learn from the history that should never be repeated. Their relevance to what we do now and how we conduct ourselves as a society is represented in the objects that teach and remind us of our history. To destroy them will not change that history and will not bring anyone back. But, to destroy an object in an attempt to push a left wing agenda or to rehash hatred of days gone by, is a childish and counter-productive method of teaching our future leaders how not to act or behave when the subject becomes a political hot topic.

A well-known veteran of WWII and Korea in the Bloomsburg, PA area named Dick Donald, once gave a presentation which myself and Sgt. Libby were asked to attend on his experiences at Iwo Jima. He was present in the Battle of Iwo Jima and witnessed, with his own eyes the raising of the American flag which is now the iconic photograph. Dick displayed a multitude of items that were his during the war and spoke about each of them.

He actually had his issued *"cricket clicker"* that made a type of clicking sound to identify himself to other American soldiers in the dark so as to not be shot by friendly fire and help with locating their positions. He held it up and asked the crowd if they knew what it was and to my amazement, only a few people had a clue as to what it was. Myself having just watched an old black and white movie about the battles there, knew what it was for and found it to be exciting to have heard a soldier that was actually there and allow us to hear the sound that would have been heard by the American and enemy soldiers alike.

After the demonstration and lecture, I approached him and asked him this, *"Dick, I know that the cricket is old and that you have had it for many years. I personally understand the importance it played in your time there and that you have taken great care of it all of these years. But, can I please hold it and possibly click it myself."* He looked at me, smiled and allowed me to do so. Now, I know it is a small dime-store trinket to many, but to the soldiers that served on Iwa Jima, it saved their lives many times and for Dick it was no exception. I was honored to have seen it, held it and even operated this simple tool of the American soldiers. Without it's preservation, the story would loose some of it's *zing*, if you will. Thank you Dick for your brave service, your continued pursuit in educating others, your display of faith in Jesus Christ and your preservation of these important artifacts we all can learn from. Just another example of how important it is to preserve history!

This section will provide some history and truth about several items that Sgt. Libby has preserved from the days of his youth, the CCC Camps as well as serving in WWII. Enjoy this section that we had previously thought of placing in **From The Command Car**, but decided to save it for this follow-up book. Also, while looking at these items, ask yourself if tearing down a statue of a Civil War general or a figure from a controversial period of American history will teach you and be a productive battle to fight. Or, will it be best served to place a well thought out plaque near it which tells of how we can and should all learn more about what our country went though to become so great a nation.

Polish-made pistol taken from German soldier in shakedown and presented to Libby by Captain Jones. 9 mm Vis 35 Radom. *Photo 2017 by Steve Hunter.*

In *From The Command Car*, Sgt. Libby spoke about an interrogation of some German soldiers that had just fired upon an American tank and killed the boys inside. After an American soldier lost his cool in the questioning, feeling the hurt of our boys being killed at the hands of these particular German soldiers, this souvenir was gifted to Sgt. Libby for his heroics and driving skills which flushed them out of a huge hedgerow that this particular section of forest which was famous for hiding German snipers.

Sgt. Libby considers this one of his prize possessions since it was gifted to him by Captain Jones who he had such tremendous respect for and found it an honor to drive him into battle. He has had many offers to buy the gun from the many people who have heard the story and quickly responds, *"no thank you"* to the cash offers for such a piece of history. Someday, this weapon will belong to a museum and appreciated by the many onlookers with this great story attached to this important piece of WWII history, but for now, the pistol is locked tightly away in a bank safety deposit box.

HERE IS THE ACTUAL STORY PULLED OUT
OF *FROM THE COMMAND CAR* . . .

A Sherman tank approached Charles's command car that had just came back from the rear echelon in the ordinance area. This tank from the 3rd Armored Division was manned by a Tech Sgt. Driver, a 1st Lieutenant and another Sergeant. Libby and the other boys in the area met the tank driver along the roadside and went over to give them an important message about what they may find ahead. The report was that there were some German soldiers still hiding in a thick hedgerow near an old farmhouse ahead to the left of the actual tank battle that was still going hot and heavy. Sgt. Libby recalls the important instructions they told these young tankers and tells it as if it was yesterday.

```
The three GI's came back from ordinance
and we told them that there was still some
Germans up there in the hedgerow. They were
full of piss and vinegar and were sort of
smug with us. Captain Jones told them to be
very careful and spray it good with machine
gun fire to get them out of there before
we would all have to pass through. About
fifteen minutes later we heard the loud and
all too familiar blast of a bazooka. We knew
right away that those sons-of-b's hit that
tank! It was only a few minutes later that
the tank driver came back toward us in the
crippled tank and crying . . . C. Libby
```

The distraught tank driver was sobbing and told the men of the 628th that the Germans had hit his tank with a bazooka shell and that his boys inside were both dead! After the tank driver described what had just happened, Captain Jones asked Charles to aid in the removal of the two bodies. He also asked Peterson to radio for an ambulance to take the bodies back to the rear echelon and be properly taken care of. At that point Captain Jones asked the tank driver if he wanted him to contact his unit to tell them what happened. Captain Jones personally took the radio and contacted the proper units to tell of this terrible misfortune which befell the two American soldiers.

> I climbed up on the tank and looked down into the space and saw that the two soldiers were lying there dead, at least what was left of them. I had to reach down in there and both of my arms immediately got covered with blood. I started to pull the first soldier out by grabbing under his arms but had to stop for a moment to slide his head back over into the correct position. His face was gone and I was trying to make sure that I had his whole body when I pulled him out of the tank. When I lifted the second soldier out, we had to slide the top of his head over that was almost cut all the way off from the shrapnel. For several days, that was all I could think about. It was terrible! . . . C. Libby

When the sad chore of loading the dead into an ambulance was finished, Captain Jones showed the most emotion to that point that Charles had ever seen from him. He told Charles in a stern manner to get into the command car. Not only Charles loaded up to go after the Germans, but several of the men of the 47th Armored Infantry climbed on top of the vehicle to go and aid in this mission to hunt down these murderers.

```
He told me to get in the vehicle and told
me, Lets go get those bastards! The 47th
guys were hanging all over my vehicle. They
knew where we were going and they wanted to
help to take them out. Captain Jones didn't
say much but I could tell by his expres-
sion that he was pissed off and really meant
business . . . C. Libby
```

As Charles reached the area, instead of driving along the side of the hedge-row, he used quick thinking and capitalized on his own sadness and anger by driving straight into the heavy brush to flush them out. When they heard the large vehicle coming straight toward them, four German soldiers fled the thick hedgerow with their hands held up high in the air yelling, "*Comrade, Comrade!*" All of the men of the 47th Armored Infantry who had climbed onto the command car immediately jumped off of and took the four Germans as prisoners or war. Captain Jones exited the vehicle and spoke to another vehicle driver who had approached after seeing the commotion in the hedgerow. The 47th began their tough interrogation with the men and made it short, sweet and to the point . . .

```
I was watching all of them from my vehicle.
They were near a farmhouse now standing
with their hands up in the air. I could
hear one of the soldiers who was talking to
them start yelling, you guys only surrender
when you run out of bazooka shells! At that
point, in one smooth motion, the soldier
fired in a straight line once to the right
and once to the left with automatic fire
across the bodies of the German soldiers
killing them where they stood! When they
were dead, the guys searched their bodies
```

to find anything that would give us information about the other German troops in the
area . . . C. Libby

Captain Jones knew that the anger of these men was high and that what they
did to these soldiers was a justified move and without time to take prisoners during a heated battle which was going on just a few miles from this
particular situation, he turned a blind eye and the men went back to their
staging area until it was safe enough for all of them to move forward into
the city of Bastogne.

Captain Jones had gone over to the bodies himself and took a pistol from one of
the dead soldiers. He walked toward the
vehicle and yelled to me, here Libby and
threw me his pistol in its hard leather
case. I still have it today and consider it
one of my prized possessions. I guess that
Captain Jones thought the way I drove into
the hedgerow without any fear was a good
move that led us to finding those German
soldiers. As we were getting ready to leave,
one of the guys of the 47th climbed back
onto the vehicle and said to me, Now, they
are good German soldiers . . . C. Libby

This particular pistol is a *9mm Vis 35 Radom* which was made in Poland.
Vis, in Latin, means *power* and was a work-horse of a pistol and still is
to this day. When the Germans took the country of Poland in 1939,
they captured the Radom factory and used it toward supplying these pistols for the Nazi army. The Vis 35 was later slightly redesigned into the
German P-35. The Germans literally made thousands of these to issue
to their soldiers.

I thought that I had heard all of his stories upon the completion of our first book. I thought that I had seen and held all of the souvenirs that he has preserved from his time spent in the war. But, one day I was blessed with a new story and a new piece of gear that was very special to him which I had not yet seen and actually had overlooked many times over.

Being an avid hunter to this day, Sgt. Libby takes great pride and a special interest in the game animals that freely walk around his home and property on a daily basis. In his life he has harvested deer in both Pennsylvania and in Germany. He fished for trout and even hunted smaller game like squirrels, rabbits and pheasant.

I went his home to have him sign a box of books that just arrived along with my two daughters, Michelle and Angelina. We found Sgt. Libby at the kitchen window looking across a corn field with a large pair of binoculars that looked to be something of a military style. They were still in great working condition but looked to have some age to them. I set the box of books down on his kitchen table as I overheard Sgt. Libby talking to my daughters. Deep in the heart of a story that I did not find familiar, I quickly spoke up and said, "*Start over Mr. Libby, I'm not sure I know this story*". He looked at me and said, "*Really, I never told you about these artillery field glasses?*" We moved to the kitchen table where we have many times, made ourselves comfortable as he started to share this new story with me. I started to make notes and get the full grasp of how and where he acquired these binoculars or as he referred to them, field artillery glasses.

He explained to me that the 628th was located in Witzenhausen, Germany. While sitting in his command car waiting for the orders to advance, Sgt. Libby noticed a man pushing a cart coming up from the direction that the battle was going on with several things stacked on it. One thing that caught his attention were two wooden boxes. Not out of the ordinary, but these boxes were marked with the sign of the Nazis, the *swastika*. To Sgt. Libby, being a vigilant observer, this was a red flag and prompted him to take a closer inspection of the contents in these two boxes.

The radio man, Peterson, said to Charles, "*Why don't you get down and see what he has?*"

Charles jumped down from his vehicle and instructed the man to stop in German. It turns out that the man was actually a former German POW of Polish descent. Sgt. Libby further describes that moment.

I asked him what was in the boxes and he answered me in German that it didn't matter. I reached back to my hip for my pistol and he quickly stopped because he knew then that I meant business. I began to inspect the entire cart and found clothes and uniforms of German soldiers. They were really of no concern to me but the boxes had the Nazi symbol on them and that caused me some concern that it could be weapons or bombs. I opened the first box. It was gray with black felt lining separating 12 pairs of artillery field glasses. The second box was exactly the same with 12 more in it. I took a pair out and held it up into the air and said to Peterson, look here! He said, how many are there and I told him that the box was filled and threw a pair to him. I took another for myself and before I could think to lift the box into my armored car, a soldier from the 109th infantry division overheard me and came to see what I had. He called some of his guys over to see them as well and like a bunch of vultures grabbing the last scrap of meat, they were all gone! I should have thought quicker to get a pair

```
for Colonel Cole to have on the vehicle as
well but it all happened so darned fast.
I'm still upset that I didn't get a pair for
him that day . . . C. Libby
```

Knowing that the items would have been given over to the Provost Marshall, he didn't complain and got out of there with the two pair of brand new field artillery glasses that enabled both he and Peterson to see for a long distance when needed in battle or to look down a long road.

```
After that, I told the man in German to move
on. He picked up his cart and moved down
the road. As we advanced, that was all I saw
of him. I still have the artillery glasses
and they are in pretty good shape for being
so old. I see a lot of deer and turkey with
them all the time! . . . C. Libby
```

They are a heavy piece of gear to carry around but are a great representation of the expert craftsmanship that the Germans prided themselves in making their military gear. Almost 75 years old and they still work great and are still useful to the former command car driver now for his personal enjoyment.

So, this is the story that prompted me to sit Sgt. Libby down once again and ask him if he thought he'd have enough energy to do another book with me. He looked at me and he said . . .

```
I don't think you would have enough in-
formation to do another book . . . would
you? . . . C. Libby
```

I told him between this story and all the other information that I learned during our book speeches, we had more than enough for a follow up. He smiled and said to me, *"Let's do it!"* So here we are with Sgt. Libby — 100 Years of Stories! The rest as they say, is history!

Field glasses put to use for deer instead of German soldiers. *Photo 2017 by Steve Hunter.*

The brainwashing of the German youth was a part of the war that the American soldiers had to learn the hard way. Never in a million years would they had thought that they would not only have to dodge bullets from the many German adult soldiers but that they would also be dodging attacks from the German youth they would encounter. The Hitler Youth was a program initiated by the Nazi Party long before Hitler had started his full advance across the European landscape. His plans for these young children to someday become soldiers to protect the motherland, was a diabolical scheme that ended up killing both many American and British soldiers and forced many of our soldiers into killing young German children.

The history of this twisted, sickening and methodical practice can be researched and learned about in many historical resources. We choose to pray for the souls of those misguided children that had no idea that the man that was praising them and rewarding their bad behavior was the devil himself!

The very act of taking an innocent life and making them horrible monsters is something that adds just one more to the list of things that Hitler did to make him one of the worst evil-doers that ever walked the face of this planet.

A Nazi Youth armband was preserved by Sgt. Libby as a terrible part of what he saw during his time fighting the Nazis. It was obtained during the war prior to the occupation from a house that he was inspecting as a part of routine shakedowns to find those who would sympathize with the Nazi's. They would regularly uncover guns, radios and other items that could be used in many ways against the US and other Allied Forces. The item seemed to be unworn and probably was from one of their sons or just a piece of history that the locals were saving for themselves. Sgt. Libby never found out but knew that this souvenir was one to grab and bring home to the US to show his family exactly what he faced while in the war. We chose not to display the armband due to many bad memories of the young children he saw slaughtered during that time of war.

A small book written and illustrated by two soldiers in 1945 depicting the journey of an American GI from his quiet and peaceful life in the states through the less peaceful times of the war. Entitled, *Who Me?*, several drawings and a story of how the Japanese bombed Pearl Harbor and he enlisted to go and fight in Europe against the Germans. Brief summaries of his travels through basic training in the US maneuvers, take you back in time as to what they endured. Sketches of soldiers hanging their heads over the side of a boat transporting them to their fate in Europe show the humorous side of a soldier's life. Darker pictures of soldiers entering the Hurtgen Forest depict the horrible days spent there as our GI's are shown fighting in the cover of the trees. A complete summary in pictures of the darker days of WWII to take home to share with relatives and friends to help put things into some type of a perspective.

A simply made book, but a great tribute to the many trials our brave men were cast into during those times. Sgt. Libby remembers getting this upon his return home and has kept it in perfect condition for all these years and mentions how it helped his mother and father understand just what he was through for the past four years upon his return.

The Prayer Book and Hymnal of Sgt. Libby's late mother are two additions to the collection that were just recently given to him by a family member, Carol Evans. Carol is the daughter of Sgt. Libby's sister Dorothy and had kept them safe for all these years. At a recent family reunion, Carol blessed Sgt. Libby with some items that he could not wait to share with me for this book. These gifts with the hand- written dedication to his mother and dated 1906 are special to him and when held in his hands, you can see the love he still holds for his mother and how much these souvenirs mean to him.

A small book entitled School Day Autobiography is another of the more recent items that was gifted to Sgt. Libby by his niece Carol Evans. Faded letters embossed into the cover, this old family possession is now back in the hands of Sgt. Libby. Belonging to his sister Dorothy June Libby, it is dated 1915. Prior to Charles being born, the book was carried to each of her school years and recorded the teachers she had, the classes she attended and many addresses and special messages from students she attended school with.

Charles was no exception to signing his sister's book on November 4th of 1930. The message, reads as such . . . "*Dear sister, If you take a pill before each day, it will carry a pain away.*" Signed your brother Charles A. Libby. When I asked him about this funny inscription he wrote all of those years ago and how it came about, he replied . . .

```
I have no idea why I wrote that. I did joke
often with my sister, but that was a lot of
years ago. It has faded away from my head
and I really don't remember why I wrote that
silly phrase . . . C. Libby
```

I wrote what he said, but I can see the wheels turning in his mind as to why he may have written what he did to his sister. I am quite sure that one day, or in the middle of the night, I will receive a telephone call with the complete explanation as to why this message was in there. I do know that when I see him reach back into his memory banks concerning his sister, it is a very pleasant memory that always places a big smile on his face with a sense of sadness that she is gone.

Coins, necklaces and many other trinkets were found all over the many battlefields on the path of the 628th. An easy pick-up and drop in the pocket kind of souvenir that many of our soldiers brought back to share with their family and friends. Sgt. Libby picked up quite a few along his travels through Germany during that time, small souvenirs that remind him of his buddies all trying to get rich by gathering up as much currency as they could to change in the money exchanging office prior to shipping home.

```
Malvestuto had pockets full of money and gave
it away like candy. When we told him that he
could change most of it for American curren-
cy, he almost started crying! . . . C. Libby
```

A pocket watch is another saved item that young Charles carried with him during his time in the CCC Camp, Camp Morton, one of the few items that he carried in his pockets during that time. After asking him what he may have carried in his pockets as a youngster, he quickly answered,

```
I used to carry a pocket watch and I
still have it. And, it still works! Wanna
see it? . . . C. Libby
```

He was very proud of that watch and immediately stood up from our interview and led me to his bedroom where he had it proudly placed in a drawer full of small trinkets that he has saved over the past 100 years. Nothing of any monetary value, but to him they are valuable in rich memories of his youth and days gone by traveling around with General Patton and the boys of either the CCC Camps or the 628th Tank Destroyer Battalion. The watch was purchased at a small pawn shop in Williamsport, Pa prior to going off to the CCC Camp for almost nothing but today it represents a special time in his life and a value can not be placed on that.

The next special souvenir is not one that Sgt. Libby brought back from his time in the war. It wasn't taken from a German soldier or recovered from the battlefield. In fact, it was something that was given to him upon his return home. Sgt. Libby's mother gave this knife to him after he got home as a sort of *I'm proud of you* gift. It was actually something that she had saved for quite some time and felt that now was a good time to pass it on to her son that she was so proud of for his military service.

The knife itself has a bone handle and is made very well. To this day, I myself would have no problem either using it for a hunting accessory or to use it in actual combat or self defense. The craftsmanship is excellent and it feels very good in your hand. The case shows a little wear, but is still in great condition. Sgt. Libby explains more about this prize family heirloom . . .

```
My mother gave me this knife one day, short-
ly after I returned home from the war. She
told me that it was mine now and was happy
to give it to me. It was handmade by my
great grandfather. It was special to her
and I was glad she gave it to me and not my
older brother. I have kept it put away for
all these years and wanted to share it for
the new book . . . C. Libby
```

Being that the knife was a possession of his great grandfather, it could very well date back to somewhere around the year 1850 – 1860. What a treasure and what a nice gesture for a mother to give her son this family history. During the war itself, he did carry a handmade knife that he spoke about in the first book that was made by another family member. Sgt. Libby commented about the knife . . .

> If I had been given that knife before I went to war, I may have taken that one with me also if I had it then. I'm not sure what ever happened to the one I actually carried with me during the war . . . C. Libby

The shadowboxes which contain the medals and badges received by Sgt. Libby from WWII.
Photo 2017 by Steve Hunter.

WWII medals, badges, insignia's and other items that donned the uniform of a soldier are a sign of hard work and pride. Many of these represent the best of the best, the extreme hardships they faced, the death they caused, the pain and injuries they suffered as well as pride in where they served their distinguished military careers.

Sgt. Libby was no exception to having received his share of service medals and badges. Pictured above are the ones that he keeps within the protected confines of shadow boxes. They were both professionally done for him by a friend who worked with the VA Office and he is proud to display them and share the story behind each of them with eager listeners and readers alike. As well as the rank and proper insignia of TEC5 Sgt., this is the list of his awarded military accomplishments . . .

EUROPEAN AFRICAN MIDDLE-EASTERN CAMPAIGN MEDAL WITH 4 BRONZE STARS

This particular medal was presented to Mr. Libby for his participation in the European theater during WWII and he is permitted to wear the 4 bronze service stars on the medal itself. **Good Conduct Medal**

This particular medal was presented to Sgt. Libby for more than three consecutive years of "honorable and faithful" service without any form of non-judicial punishment, disciplinary infractions or court martial offenses. It is one of the oldest military medals and the one that makes Sgt. Libby the most proud.

HONORABLE SERVICE MEDAL

This particular medal was presented to Sgt. Libby for his honorable service and sacrifices during time spent in WWII.

Victory Medal WWII
This particular medal was presented to Sgt. Libby for his active duty in Europe during WWII during the appropriate time frame of the final allied victory.

Army of Occupation WWII Medal
This particular medal was presented to Sgt. Libby for recognition of his service during the occupation period in Germany for which he performed his duties with honor.

American Defense Service Medal
This particular medal was presented to Sgt. Libby for his service before America's entry into WWII during the initial years of the European conflict.

American Campaign Medal
This particular medal was presented to Sgt. Libby for his service performed in the American Theater of Operations during WWII.

Sub-Machine Gun Badge
This particular badge was presented to Sgt. Libby for his skillful qualification of becoming a sharpshooter on the military shooting range.

Sgt. Libby received his medals many years after the war at the aid of someone from the local Veterans Administration. He did not leave Germany with his unit due to being badly burned just before his time of occupation was over. He never got the chance to stand with his fellow tankers and have them pinned on his uniform. He never had the fanfare of hundreds of appreciative onlookers cheering as he was awarded these medals. But, his recognition is now a part of his entire life within this set of books about his life and his service.

**Inscribed on the back, Honored WWII Veteran
November 12, 2005.** *Photo 2017 by Steve Hunter.*

Local WWII gathering and recognition award . . . Sgt. Libby is very proud of his community and all of the veterans that have come from the same area. Many of his friends served in WWII and also had great stories to tell and share with others. Many would not talk about what they experienced and many passed away long ago taking this great information along with them before it could be properly documented. What a sad thing to imagine and what a blessing it would have been for all of it to be told and properly preserved.

On November 12, 2005, many WWII Veterans were invited to a large gala at The Capital Theater in his hometown of Williamsport, PA to all be honored for their outstanding service and for organizers of this event to show the the communities appreciation for these veterans. A medal was given to each of the men as they were announced and each accepted this honor with pride and sadness alike. Between each of the recipients receiving their awards, many spoke to one another, exchanging comments and short stories.

Sgt. Libby was no exception and leaned forward to a 1st Lieutenant and a Captain sitting in the seats in front of him. Sgt. Libby shares the comments as such. . .

```
I leaned forward and asked them both, I
bet you guys probably saw a lot of action.
The Captain leaned back and said in a mean
voice, "Yeah, but we don't want to talk about
it!" I spoke back to him and said, well I
do! I want others to know what happened
and what I went through! They turned their
heads and no more words were spoken between
these particular men . . . C. Libby
```

THE MISSING MEDAL

As I had previously listed in our first book, *From The Command Car*, Sgt. Libby was awarded several medals for his service within WWII. I have seen them on several occasions, photographed them and helped to carry them to our presentations for others to see and appreciate. I look at them and realize just how important it is to these soldiers in their later years to be recognized for their days as younger men and for what they had done.

It came to me one day that maybe, just maybe, there may be some medals that were overlooked for Sgt. Libby so I began to research what medals were available to a man that served in the US Army, his ranking, his job specifications, his time spent in the European Theater of Operations and anything else I could think of or find within this new research project.

In all the searching, there was one medal that I investigated a little more to see if it was possible for him to claim this as his final medal for his service during WWII. The medal I refer to is called **The Soldiers Medal**. The soldiers medal is awarded to those soldiers who have served with heroics and had a hand in the saving of lives. After this research, I quickly began to compile a list of circumstances that fit this award and sent it off to the VA where our local director, George Heiges, directed me to the proper forms to formerly apply with to our Congressman.

My application was submitted and I waited for their decision. Within my first petition, I finished the six chosen occasions and stories with these simple comments. . .

> *During combat, the responsibilities of a command car driver place him in the most dangerous spots at all times. He and he alone, many times, saves lives by the direction he drives and the actions he takes. Driving a commanding officer to locations to observe troop movements, transport soldiers to the lines as well as the evasive maneuvers that are a specialty of such a driver, are all life-saving moments that go unnoticed by many.*
>
> *This and all the other examples of heroism are why I believe that TEC5 Sgt. Charles A. Libby deserve The Soldiers Medal.*
>
> *Thank you for your time and I look forward to your responses and the planning of awarding this 100 year old WWII Veteran something that is long overdue.*

So, without any knowledge of my doing this for him, we are now waiting for the final approval from the Pennsylvania government to confirm his eligibility for this honor. When the day comes that he is presented with this medal, we will post photos on his website fromthecommandcar.com and the From The Command Car Facebook page. What an exciting period of time it is waiting for the news to come in about this final award that he will qualify for.

Recently, we spoke about medals and a story that he tells often is a source of pain to him. Not bragging about how many medals he received, but about how he didn't get to come back to the states along with his fellow C-Company boys.

I got burned badly over in England while
trying to do my laundry. I had to stay in
a hospital to recover and couldn't get back
to the states with the other guys. They were
well received as their ship pulled up into
the harbor in New York. I heard that they had
hundreds of people there cheering for them
and thanking them for what they had just done.
By the time I got back to the states, some of
the excitement had died down and there were
only a few people there to greet us. They got
a parade, confetti and girls kissing all of
them, I came home with scars on my arms and
it seemed like it was just back to trying to
get work and coming home like any normal day
of the week . . . C. Libby

This is another reason why I do what I do for him. I truly feel that all veterans who serve honorably should be shown the same respect that those other soldiers had gotten during the days of parades and crowds of people cheering for them. Upon receiving this final medal from WWII, we will celebrate and honor him properly and place photos on his website for all to enjoy.

Another medal that he speaks of with sadness is the medal that a French veteran of WWI presented to hi on a war-torn road at the time they liberated a German occupied city. This French man approached the young GI and speaking in French, and handing him his medal that he was presented with upon finishing his service in WWI. The appreciation of the people was overwhelming and this man's gratitude was proven by giving the young Charles his most valuable possession.

The Germans ransacked our make-shift base
camp and took all of our stuff. They got my

```
ruck sack, my wallet, cash, some other stuff
I had in there that I was going to recover
when we fell back from the battle. The big-
gest thing they got from me was the medal
that the French man gave to me. That was
very important to him and I am so sorry that
the Germans got it. It meant a lot to me to
have gotten it and to this day, I still re-
gret leaving it in my pack for those Germans
to get it! . . . C. Libby
```

Pride in his service, pride for his country and compassion for those who also endured the hardships of a war that was fought not too long before he stepped foot on their soil. Regrets, pain, memories and a lifetime of looking back on what happened to him as a soldier fighting in the battles of WWII. There truly is no medal that can be placed on the chest of a soldier that can equal the sacrifices they made and continue to make while wearing the uniform of United Stated soldier. God Bless them all.

As a writer, I have spoken to many veterans that have mixed emotions when telling their stories. Many that have seen death don't want to relive it by describing what they saw. Many can not bear to relive it by diving deep into their subconscious and seeing those images once again. On the other hand, many understand the value of explaining such stories as a form of therapy and it helps them to sort out many things that bothered them long ago. Everyone is different, but everyone had similar experiences like fear, sadness and death that they had to endure during those times and still, long after it all happened. God bless them!

This Garrison hat was worn by Sgt. Libby during his photos and formal events during WWII. He kept this treasure wrapped up and protected for over 70 years! The photo on the cover of *From The Command Car* shows this exact hat in it's pristine condition. To recapture the look and show the comparison of the young Sgt. Libby and the now 100 year old Sgt. Libby, he pulled it out for us to enjoy a newer photo of him wearing the hat on his 100th birthday.

100 years old and it still fits! *Photo 2017 by Steve Hunter.*

Sgt. Libby enjoys his regular appearances at parades, book signings, speeches and other veteran events. During these events, whether in full WWII uniform or not, he always wears one of these hats to signify his service and time in WWII. He wears these hats with pride and enjoys telling what each of the patches or pins stands for which are proudly displayed on the hat itself.

Service hats worn by Sgt. Libby at his many events and special occasions. *Photo 2017 by Steve Hunter.*

The families of soldiers who were serving in WWII kept their family member in prayer and wanted others to know that they were proud to have someone close to them serving our great country during these scary times. A service flag with a blue star was proudly displayed in the window to recognize their being over seas and was only changed to a gold star if their relative had been killed in action.

Once again, Carol Evans came to the call of returning this family heirloom to Sgt. Libby for use in the book ad as a loving memory of how his mother missed and wanted him to return home unscathed. Along with his Letter of Protection, his faith and the service flag hanging in his home in Pennsylvania, Sgt. Libby did come home unscathed and very proud of his service!

This tradition continues still today and is a fitting tribute and constant reminder of just how important each of these men and women who are serving mean to all of us!

The actual Blue Star Flag that was placed within the Libby Family window as Sgt. Libby served in WWII. *Photo 2017 by Steve Hunter.*

Like most collectors, Sgt. Libby finds great pleasure in items that take him back to family and his childhood. A hand-carved pecan pit bracelet takes him back to the days of sitting and watching his grandfather use his many gifts and talents to produce beautiful items. A handy man by trade and machinist of the time, the young Charles would sit and watch him in his spare time carve assorted items. This perfectly preserved bracelet shows how his grandfather was blessed with the vision to make a normally thrown away piece of left over food scrap into something that has lasted for over 80 years.

Unknown who's license it had been back in 1917, but a reminder of the year he was born and the fact that he had a drivers license early in his teens which made him qualified to become a command car driver when he entered the tank unit so long ago. A keep-sake of the past and an important memory to this former command car driver.

What do you collect? What is it that triggers happy memories that you insist on keeping around you? Whatever it may be, remember the significance and the importance to you at this time and think of how it may be important to future generations to come. Preserve both the item and a written recall of why you saved it. Details may end up in a book just like this someday when someone sees it's value and you will be that much richer within your heart for knowing that others appreciate it as you have.

The Book Tour, Events and The Press

* * *

BEING THRUST INTO THE SPOTLIGHT of recognition and admiration by many for anyone, at any age, is something that takes getting used to. For a man in his late 90's, 98 to be more accurate, it seemed as if Sgt. Charles Libby had been preparing for this day for many many years. From the moment that I placed the first copy into his hands and said, *"Here we go!"* it was off and running for this WWII hero to share his stories with the masses.

```
Steve told me that the publisher would not
allow my photo on the front cover. He told
me that he tried but they wouldn't allow it.
When he handed me the book and I saw the
photo I wished to have on there, I looked
at him and said you so and so. He sure got
one over on me! He kept that a secret for a
long time . . . C. Libby
```

The book tour, the many speeches, the autographs within the inner cover of his book, *From The Command Car*, the newspaper articles, the radio interviews and a few spots on local television stations, all have been quite a ride of excitement and privilege for this WWII hero. The press has been very kind to the both of us on this journey and we thank them all for their kindness.

With some of the normal stages of aging taking place within the body of this WWII veteran, Sgt. Libby has some trouble with the pointer finger on his left hand which he writes with. Signing many autographs at times is a difficult process due to the stiffness that has set in. He gives it his best shot and responds to the eager autograph seekers with this apology . . .

```
My finger is bent now cause I'm older. Also,
the moisture in my hands is not there any-
more so it's hard for me to write. It may
not look to neat, but I'll do my best . . .
C. Libby
```

I myself am a collector of autographs as many people are. I have some that I have collected over the years that if I had not done some sort of reference, I would not know who's it was. In my opinion, Sgt. Libby does a fine job and it looks like the signature of a man that has experience, years on him and is very legible. He likes for me to bring the boxes of books to him prior to an event so that he can take his time and sign them privately. He's getting pretty good at it now! He enjoys having them finished so that he can spend his time telling stories at his events and not having to sign as many books in person.

He was shocked when I told him that many school-aged children are not learning cursive and proper hand writing like we both did in our school days.

```
How the heck are kids going to write their
names? I hate to see kids getting lazy and
not learning important things that they
need in life . . . C. Libby
```

In the beginning of the tour at the release of *From The Command Car*, I started the process by contacting the local newspapers to write a blurb or two about the book to get some local exposure. The response was overwhelming! The Williamsport Sun-Gazette's, Cara Morningstar, did a special feature on the book along with many others in our area and did fantastic write-ups bringing *From The Command Car* into the spotlight. There are so many others to mention that I want to just thank all of them for their professionalism and overwhelming support.

A local radio DJ named John Finn on WZXR, invited Sgt. Libby into the studio for a show entitled *In Touch*. The show focuses on people that have interesting stories to tell about their lives. Sgt. Libby was more than anxious to speak and John was more than excited to hear some of his stories. This also got him warmed up for his next adventure which was a featured television spot on a show called PA Live.

Television was a little nerve racking for Sgt. Libby and he seemed to have harder time with that format. But, a pat on the back, a big smile from the beautiful host of the show, Amy Kehm and then he loosened up to tell her a little about his time spent during WWII following General Patton around Europe.

Jokes to the audience in the early days about being nervous . . . *"If you hear anything knocking, that's just my knees"*, quickly gained laughs from the audience and helped to relax this WWII veteran. As his book signings became more frequent, the knees stopped knocking and the nerves seemed to settle down while getting up in front of the many large crowds. Jokes about how he looked like Errol Flynn as a young man as well as his dancing prowess were all hits at these events.

Local libraries were the first to snatch myself and Mr. Libby up for presentations. The Union County Library in Lewisburg, PA and the JV Brown Library in Williamsport, PA were two of the first to do so. Church groups, historical society meetings as well as the Brass Pelican Restaurant located in Benton, PA where Sgt. Libby spent time while serving in the CCC Camp Morton, also jumped at the chance to have him speak about his days in the CCC Camp and his time spent in WWII.

The Lycoming County Helping Our Warriors, based in Williamsport, PA, also invited Mr. Libby and myself to speak and to have books on hand for eager readers. This event held at the same armory that Sgt. Libby had initially joined the service, was a big reminder to many of how many veterans from this area of Pennsylvania joined, trained and served for this wonderful country that we live in. Funds from this event helped to take care of expenses that suffering veterans need to either pick up their lives or start their lives over after unfortunate events. Information to help this great caring organization can be found in the sponsorship section at the end of this book. Please support them! Grand Marshall of a parade is the most honored position of that type of event. It gives honor and pays tribute to a person for their specialized accomplishments. Sgt. Libby, since the release of his life story in *From The Command Car*, has been asked to be the Grand Marshall of two separate veteran parades and had been asked to perform that duty prior to the books release as well. The first for us was in Muncy, PA for the local VFW and their 2016 Annual Memorial Day Parade. The parade complete with a PT Boat (*patrol torpedo*), jeeps, cars, other military vehicles and marching bands, made it's way through many streets and eventually ended up in a large cemetery where several US Veterans are at their final resting spots.

Prior to the parade, Sgt. Libby was greeted by a news crew that interviewed him for the local television station and followed us throughout the parade capturing glimpses of him waiving to the crowd of applauding parade-goers. The coverage was exciting for Sgt. Libby and it sparked something within him that brought out a realization of just how special he is to the many people who know him and many others who respect him for what he did for this country long ago.

Sgt. Fred Agnoni, a Korean War Veteran, drove Sgt. Libby and myself through this parade in his red Mustang, eventually delivering us at the cemetery where we were both asked to speak to the large crowd that followed the parade. I opened the speaking with a speech on how parents should remove the cell phone from their children's hands, get them away from the video games and bring them to places like this in an effort to teach them about their freedoms and how these freedoms are not free at all! The speech came with warm and appreciative response from the crowd and hit a nerve with many as to the condition of our country's ability at that time under the serving administration in Washington didn't always properly honor these great men and women.

Sgt. Libby also spoke to the crowd, delivering some wonderful stories from his time in WWII to a standing ovation and had many eager parade-goers wanting to have their photos taken with this real life WWII hero.

Lewisburg, PA was the site of the second parade that we were asked to be a part of and Sgt. Libby once again was asked to be their 2016 Grand Marshall. **The Union County Veterans' 4th of July Parade** is one of the largest, if not the largest, in the Eastern United States. Nearing year 25 of hosting this event, their motto is *"One Nation . . . Communities United."* It is well worth the trip each year to come and see this fantastic event that takes an entire year of preparing for the upcoming year's parade and weekend of exciting and educational activities.

Our mutual friend and parade committee member, Barb Spaventa, called me one night and said that she was at a meeting for the parade and the topic of discussion was who was going to be the Grand Marshall. She asked me if Sgt. Libby would be interested in doing this for the 2016 event and assured me that it would be something big and that Sgt. Libby would be treated like royalty for the weekend. We were not disappointed!

Displays of Vietnam era helicopters were on hand, past and current military personnel as well as a wide variety of military armament and equipment. The parade that lasts longer than any I have ever witnessed with actual veterans and dozens of reenactment soldiers from the periods of the Revolutionary War, the Civil War, WWI, WWII, Korean War, Vietnam War and more recent wars in Iraq, Afghanistan and Kuwait. They all came out to salute our past veterans and to be saluted and honored themselves!

At the end of the parade route, hundreds gathered to hear many of these honored veterans speak. Sgt. Libby gave a powerful speech and received a standing ovation from the crowd as their 2016 Grand Marshall which gave him great pleasure and stirred up many emotions.

```
I liked the WWI dough-boy outfit one fella
had on. He really looked like a soldier from
that war! Everyone was so nice and treated
me with respect. I guess they saw my hat
with my unit patch on it and knew that I
was the real deal and that I served under
General Patton . . . C. Libby
```

For the VIP guests the same night of the parade, they took us to a fancy gala where Sgt. Libby was honored with many special guests. We all shared a meal and great music from a live band playing music from the big band era. Sgt. Libby spoke to the select crowd of VIP's and was presented with a special bust of a soldier by the parade committee and handed to him by SGM Kevin Bittenbender which brought tears to his eyes. He proudly displays the bust in his living room for all to see.

Grand Marshal appreciation award. *Photo 2016 by Steve Hunter.*

The night was not complete without Sgt. Libby dancing with almost every woman that was in the room. The looks on the faces of those who had never seen him dance was an amazing sight to see. Shocked is an understatement! At the time, 98 ½ years young, Sgt. Libby successfully wore out all the other dancers and was still ready to dance as the band was packing up their gear. Now the next day, his legs were a little tired, but he enjoyed it so much that he would have done it all over if asked to.

One other highlight of the evening was the opportunity for the both of us to meet the grand daughter of baseball legend Babe Ruth who attended the event. She has supported this cause for many years and is a favorite there for many. Linda Ruth Tosetti spent time taking to us about her grand father and also listening to Sgt. Libby and his incredible stories. She was gracious enough to sign baseballs and photos of *The Babe* and her mother together as souvenirs for the both of us to take home. Sgt. Libby and I, both huge baseball fans, enjoyed the evening very much. There was even an appearance and speech from none other than Ben Franklin! Well, a great impersonator of the historical figure that gave great advice to the attendees. I cherish every aspect of the event and will carry the memories with me forever as well as Sgt. Libby.

For the 2017 parade in Lewisburg we had the privilege of attending, not as the Grand Marshall but as a part of the large display of authentic military vehicles. I was contacted on social media by two men that claimed to have a vehicle that they said Sgt. Libby would love to see, ride in and even drive if he wished. William Brown and Alan Rosenfeld are the proud owners of an M-20 Scout Command Car. YES! The exact vehicle that Sgt. Libby drove through the entire war. They offered to meet us anywhere we would like to not only share their unbelievable find and restoration with him, but to also get their own photos of a real life command car driver from that era posing with their prized vehicle. I really couldn't tell who was the most excited in our meeting, but I can assure all of you readers that excitement was not in short supply that day.

We decided to meet at the *2017 Union County Veterans' 4th of July Parade* and enter it into the proper military vehicle division. The look on Sgt. Libby's face as he saw the vehicle for the first time was a moment that is hard to explain. I can only imagine what a veteran feels when talking about their experiences as they relive the horrors, the excitement, the reality of the situations they faced, but to see a vehicle that is in a category of almost non-existent and to be the same type that you drove into battle, WOW! is all that can be said.

We were to meet near the parade route and as we got closer, we called William and asked where he was. As the words came out of my mouth, I saw the vehicle pulled over just ahead of us. I said to Sgt. Libby, *"There it is!"* He looked ahead much like he was seeing a long-lost friend or relative. The markings on the vehicle for identification were dedicated to Sgt. Libby by using the unit and company numbers that he served with, almost an exact replica. Soon, these men will try to duplicate the pin-up girl that was painted on the wheel fender in a final touch of honor and history to their vehicle. They wanted to honor Sgt. Libby with the markings and it's identical look and they did a tremendous job in doing so. Another example of men that understand how important this period of time was and how important it is to preserve it properly.

The M-20 Scout Command Car. *Photo 2017 credit Steve Hunter.*

It reminded me of my vehicle that I had. It seemed to be stronger than the one I had driven though. Those days, they seemed to be not built quite as well. I felt that I'd like to be out there driving it. Back then, I was good at it, but I may not have known how to drive this one we had in the parade. I really felt proud to be waiving at the people standing in that vehicle. They did a really good job restoring her and I really appreciate those two nice guys letting me ride in her. Colonel Cole would have really liked to see it as well, especially since it had all of our unit markings . . . C. Libby

Sgt. Libby never got tired of waiving during the parade, speaking out to the crowd and telling them all how he proudly served with General Patton. He also commented of how he made it through the entire war and got out alive because of the good Lord allowing him to do so. Not everyone could hear him, but he recited that through the entire parade. I smiled, clicked pictures and enjoyed the moment along with the two that brought the vehicle all the way down from New York state.

The command car seemed to be the fan favorite of the parade. How more authentic could you get with a real WWII M-20 Command Car driver on a running vehicle that is exactly like the one he drove into battle? It was an unbelievable sight to see, especially when he decided to check out the big 50 cal. gun that is mounted on the top of the vehicle, which would have been where Bik once stood back in the day ready to fire on enemy tanks and air-craft. Sgt. Libby used to stand guard as well on the same type of gun when it was his turn to stand guard and give the other guys a break. The look in his eyes while looking down the sights of the gun says it all.

Once again, special thanks to William and Alan for their love of history, their attention to detail and their desire to make wishes come true for a special WWII veteran. God Bless them both and continued success in their future preservation pieces.

Another special thanks to all who work so very hard to organize this great parade. Make sure to visit one soon to witness this great event and see all the many faces of our military being honored.

The **Endless Mountains War Museum** in Sonestown, PA is another stop that everyone should make as it is one of the best displays of war memorabilia that you could ever see! Sgt. Libby and myself have been asked several times to speak and sign books there for the war history buffs. Owner/ operator, museum president and historical preservation enthusiast, Jack Craft, has taken great care in displaying the many items you will see on hand at this private war museum. With new donations and funding in place, the museum will soon undertake a renovation to add another wing for the many items that are not able to be displayed due to the continued donations by families of soldiers who have left us.

Sgt. Libby and museum owner, Jack Craft. *Photo 2016 by Steve Hunter.*

Jack is a real nice guy. He really took a lot of time to get all of these artifacts and to preserve them for everyone to see. I enjoy my trips up there and love to talk to the people who like to listen to my stories about the second world war . . . C. Libby

Displayed in front of The Endless Mountains War Museum as a tribute to our lost soldiers.
Photo 2017 by Steve Hunter.

Here are a couple of photos of some of the displays you will see on your visit to this special place of historical military preservation. During your tour, you are blessed with the military music of the WWII era which ads to the entire experience. Goose bumps, tears and a sense of *American pride* fills your entire being as you walk the isles and rooms of displays.

Sgt. Charles Libby shaking hands with a display of the late General MacArthur.
Photo 2017 by Steve Hunter.

Authentic clothing worn by Jews in a concentration camp during the Holocaust.
Photo 2017 by Steve Hunter.

At events at the museum, we have met many veterans who provide guests with amazing stories and educate them in their field of expertise and general knowledge of their unit and branch they served in. Dick Donald and Charlie Brooking are two to mention that stood out at our times spent there at the museum. Special thanks to them for their service and for their great presentations on Iwa Jima and the PT Boats of the war. God bless you both and all that support this great museum! We were also met by some special guests that provided many feelings for Sgt. Libby and the people who traveled to meet him there alike. Having a page on Facebook for our first book ***From The Command Car***, it has provided a source of information for families to research history on past family members and who they may have served with, like Sgt. Libby. I was contacted by the family of a member of C-Company of the 628th and was shocked when I found out just who they were referring to when asking me questions about the book and the unit Sgt. Libby served with.

His message read that he had a great uncle that served in C-Company and was KIA in the Hurtgen Forest around 1944. He wanted to know if Sgt. Libby possibly knew him. Turns out, we wrote about his great uncle and friend of Sgt. Libby's in our first book! When I told him this news, he immediately told his mother and conversations began to arrange a personal meeting. The Museum was the perfect place for all of us to be able to have this first meeting and for the family and Sgt. Libby to share their stories. Debbie Taylor, niece of Louis D'iorio, her husband Fran and her son who had contacted me on Facebook, Francis, all met us there for a day of sharing stories about this tank man who gave his life during WWII. They had never met but she had heard so much about her uncle through the years from Debbie's mother and had told stories to her son alike.

D'iorio was someone that Sgt. Libby called a friend. Their friendship was not always visible on the surface, but they fought together and shared many of the same experiences that formed a bond that only soldiers can relate to.

```
Heck, we even had a fist fight once before
the war. He had a hot head and seemed like he
was always looking for a fight with someone.
One day in Camp Rucker, Alabama on maneuvers,
he pushed me when I was carrying a plate of
eggs, I dropped them and hit the corner of my
left eye on something. As I fell, I blacked
```

out for a few seconds. Well, he got my Irish
up that day and I got up and grabbed hold of
him and marched him against the wall on his
tip-toes. I started punching him in the ribs
and pushed his face into the wall. I turned
him around and started to punch him in the
belly telling him that he shouldn't have gotten my Irish up and that my grandfather said
to me that I should always take care of myself. An orderly ran into the street and announced to the entire camp what was going on.
He begged me to stop and I did but told him
that I wasn't going to take his crap anymore.
The fight ended, we shook hands and we were
still friends. The cook we all called Fat
Boy, came to me and said, "This dog-robber is
pretty good!" I guess he needed to be taught
a lesson that day and I guess that I was the
one that had to do it . . . C. Libby

When finishing the story you can see the emotions change on the face of the
now senior Sgt. Libby. Not the young boy who was facing war and his entire
life ahead of him, but the man who wishes to see all of his old friends again
and the moments that occurred between himself and others within his unit.

He was my buddy. I didn't want to fight him
and I certainly didn't want him to die there
in the Hurtgen Forest. I'm sure it has been
hard on his family . . . C. Libby

After speaking about the incident when D'iorio was killed many times, he
reflects back and now thinks that he may have been trying to find cover outside of his tank due to a fire or a big gun firing on his tank that fateful day. In
battle, there are just so many variables that rational thought at times just can

not exist. He took gun fire across his back and died for his country in that forest fighting for a cause that needed to be fought. After meeting the family of this brave soldier and hearing more about the man prior to the war, Sgt. Libby expresses his deepest sympathy to the surviving members who still look at their uncle as a hero of those tumultuous times.

He did express these final words on that particular story that he neglected to add in our last book about the KIA event of Sgt. D'iorio in the Hurtgen Forest . . .

```
I forgot to tell you something that came
into my mind about D'iorio getting killed
while running away from his tank. The other
men of his unit turned the 50 caliber on
the Germans and killed all of them that got
my friend. It wouldn't bring him back, but
in the end, they paid for it . . . C. Libby
```

Sgt. D'iorio and 1st Lt. Merz of the 628th C-Company.
Photo WWII, photographer unknown.

He presented the family with a framed photo of the two men together back in the day smiling. He also presented the family each with a Letter of Protection which we spoke of in our first book. This Letter of Protection was something that Sgt. Libby and many of the boys within C-Company carried with them into battle. Charles had taken this letter which was given to him by his mother, whose brother carried it in WWI and he shared it with many of the soldiers for them to copy. D'iorio had refused to copy the letter, dismissing it as rubbish. That day, I told the family myself that it was Mr. Libby's wish for him to have had it and he still feels that if he did have it with him that he may still be alive today. The family gladly took the letter in honor of their fallen uncle with tearful gratitude. This Letter of Protection, also referred to by Sgt. Libby as the Letter of Prayer, reads as such . . .

LETTER OF PROTECTION

```
In the name of God, the Son and The Holy
Ghost as Christ stopped at the Mount of
Olives; all guns shall stop whoever carries
this letter with him. He shall not be dam-
aged through the enemy's guns or weapons.
God will give him strength that he will not
fear robbers and murderers nor guns or pis-
tols, swords, muskets or bayonets shall not
hurt him through the command of the Father,
Son and the Holy Ghost. God be with him
whoever carries this letter with him shall
be protected against all danger and he who
doesn't believe this letter may copy it, tie
it around a dog's neck and shoot at him. He
will see it's true whoever has this letter,
shall never be taken prisoner or wounded by
the enemy as true as it is that Jesus Christ
```

```
died and ascended into Heaven and suffered
on earth. He shall stand unhurt, injured by
all guns and weapons on earth by the living
God, Son and Holy Ghost. I pray in the name
of Christ's blood that no ball shall hit
him, be it gold or silver and that God in
Heaven may deliver him from all sins in the
name of the Father, Son and The Holy Ghost.
It fell from Heaven in Palestine in 1728. It
was written in gold letters, AMEN.
```

Sgt. Libby carries several copies of this letter of protection everywhere he goes and offers it to the many people he tells his stories to. Each and every letter are always taken with great appreciation and love. I still have a copy in my wallet as a reminder of the power of protection that God himself provides to me. A copy of this letter from Sgt. Libby himself is a real treat and he encourages you to copy it for yourself as a gift from him and carry it with you just like he did through the entire war.

**Emotional presentation of WWII photo of Sgt.
Libby and Sgt. D'iorio to his family.**
Photo 2017 by Steve Hunter.

The Quilts of Valor Foundation is a nationwide organization that to date, has presented over 165,000 hand-quilted blankets and provided them to veterans in every branch of military service from WWII til more recent wars and military missions. Quilters from all across the United States contribute their talents to this great cause as way to honor our veterans.

For us, it started with a presentation that I witnessed in Danville, PA at The Maria Joseph Manor for another WWII veteran. My family and I were performing there that day and the activity director asked if we could provide a microphone and allow these people to present the quilt prior to our performance. Being that it was a patriotic theme that day and how we love our veterans, we had no trouble helping out and enjoyed the presentation very much. It prompted me to speak to Jim and Bonnie Fiedler, who came that day from the Columbia County Chapter of the organization. I began to tell them about Sgt. Libby and see if they would be willing to present him with the same type of quilt and by chance, they already knew who Sgt. Libby was and remembered me as well from hearing us speak about a year ago. They had a signed copy of *From The Command Car* and enjoyed the stories very much. Jim told me how to get in touch with the organization and properly apply, so I did as soon as I got home.

The application process is easy and requires any and all information about the veteran you are nominating for a quilt. I filled it out and was surprised at how quickly they got back to me. They understood that we had a narrowing window being that Sgt. Libby was 99 years old at the time and placed it into the expedited category. After multiple conversations, we agreed that his quilt would be presented at a big show that my family was putting on at a place called Indian Park in Montoursville, Pennsylvania on August 2, 2017.

I told Sgt. Libby about this award and presentation he eagerly agreed to be present that night in his uniform. His son, Rob Libby, brought him to the event with some WWII memories in hand for those who would like to see them. Medals, a photo of General Patton and some of his personal photos.

The show began and as the audience was just getting warmed up, I began to speak about our first book and told the audience that he was also present. I called Jim and Bonnie Fiedler up to the stage and then we announced Sgt. Libby who received a standing ovation as he approached the microphone. Nobody at this concert knew that this was planned, so they got a special treat that evening on top of the great entertainment.

The presentation of the quilt was a moving ceremony and Sgt. Libby gave a heart-filled thank you speech to the crowd while thanking the foundation for all of their hard work. As he moved back to his seat, he was flooded with audience members who wanted to meet him, shake his hand and listen to some of his stories. I can honestly say that he stole the show that night and rightfully so. It's hard to follow that act!

He carefully folded the quilt and placed it in a special bag that they also provided to him for when he was not using it. He is more than happy to show his visitors at home what he received and is very proud to be one of the recognized veterans that can say they have an authentic Quilt of Valor!

Presentation to Sgt. Libby – Quilt of Valor. *Photo 2017 by Danny Irimagha.*

The next day, Sgt. Libby was featured on the front page of *The Williamsport Sun-Gazette* for which I had to call and tell him about. He answered the telephone, still sounding excited, as I asked to speak with the celebrity that lived there. He laughed and quickly responded with his famous saying, "*That and a ham sandwich!*" I laughed and we began to relive the previous night's activities and share our stories with one another.

Thank God for these types of organizations who take time from their personal lives to gives thanks in so many ways to the great men and women who have served in our armed forces. Go to the Sponsors of History section at the end of this book and find their contact information. Take the time to elect someone, as I did, that you feel is deserving of this type of award and fill out their form to be contacted. Honor those who deserve to be honored in so many ways!

The South Williamsport Area High School in central Pennsylvania contacted me about bringing Sgt. Libby to visit for a special assembly in their large auditorium. Teacher, Karen Fink and Principal Jessie Smith took care of the details and prepared a wonderful 2017 Veterans Day Tribute and Celebration. Robyn Rummings, choral director, also organized a tribute to all branches of the military with students singing their appointed anthems. The local chapter of the Korean War Veterans Color Guard, students and educators alike, all sat and listened to the stories told by myself and Sgt. Libby.

Our format for speeches is that I set up the story and prepare Sgt. Libby for reaching back in time to capture all the emotions of the story. Students gasped, laughed and at times, sat in complete silence as they heard and witnessed this 100 year old WWII veteran share his life with them from the stage. I completed the day's event by teaching the students what they should do when meeting a veteran and how to conduct themselves in life to actually bring honor to the men and women who had given so much for all of them today!

Those kids really enjoyed my stories and
they really listened to what I said! I really liked the way they displayed that big
flag on the stage and especially enjoyed
hearing the music they prepared for all the
veterans of every branch. It was a great day
and I look forward to going back again next
year . . . C.. Libby

Special thanks to all who made that day so special for all of our veterans. It
was very satisfying for me to go back to my old school and speak from the
stage to all of those future leaders. My daughter sat in the audience and told
me when I got home how well we did which also made me proud of what I
do in my every day life.

The cover photo of this book was taken at this assembly at The South
Williamsport Area High School Auditorium. Sgt. Libby's moment of salut-
ing in front of the American flag was not only moving, but was similar to
that of George C. Scott portraying General Patton in the Hollywood movie.

The 2017 Lycoming County Annual Veterans Parade held in South
Williamsport, PA was another in a long line of events Sgt. Libby has been invited to participate in. Driven once again by our friend Freddie Agnoni and
accompanied by Parade Ambassador John Joseph Agnoni, brother of Freddie
and both subjects in my next military series book. John served in the Korean
War from 1953 – 1956 and was recognized at this event by our local VA.
We all rode together along with my daughter Angelina and were treated to
several fly-overs from two old military planes complete with smoke trailers.
Parade-goers enjoyed it s well as myself and Sgt. Libby.

Those planes reminded me of when our boys
would fly over to let us know that they were
going to take care of the Germans who we

```
were fighting up ahead. I'd look up to the
sky, salute them and tell them Thank you
boys! . . . C. Libby
```

It just keeps going on and on and on . . . the press has fallen in love with the 100 year old WWIII veteran Sgt. Libby. TV, newsprint and radio alike all have continued to give him the spotlight. Radio interviews with Backyard Broadcasting's Keith Kitchen and Eric Spencer, articles in so many newspapers I'd have to add another chapter to the book. Featured spots of him on TV in parades and other functions as well as the many events that we are booked for throughout 2018, Sgt. Libby is destined to be a household name.

THE PA HOUSE OF REPRESENTATIVES

The most recent of our events that featured an important salute to this WWII hero, took place on December 11, 2017. By the invitation of Representative Jeff Wheeland and Representative Garth Everett, myself and Sgt. Libby made our way to Harrisburg, PA to sit on the floor of the House of Representatives.

With special seats reserved by the Speaker of The House, we were escorted around the building and got the VIP tour by Rep. Wheeland's assistant Amy. Stopped by many along the way to shake the hand of Sgt. Libby, we made our way to the chambers. What a sight to see! A beautiful display of architecture and artwork blesses the entire room. Sgt. Libby and I were escorted to our seats and awaited the start of the House Session.

After the formalities of the opening prayer, the pledge and general announcements, the Speaker asked for the Sgt.-at-arms to close the doors and for all members to take their seats and to be quiet. Representatives Wheeland and Everett both took their place at the podium and Representative Wheeland read a prepared speech telling all of the respected house members the story of Sgt. Charles A. Libby. At one point, Sgt. Libby was asked to stand as members gave him a standing ovation.

Waiving and thanking them for this recognition, I could tell that he was deeply humbled by the experience. A large gasp filled the room with disbelief when the representative announced that Sgt. Libby was 100 years old.

Rep. Wheeland followed up by announcing the book *From The Command Car* and asked for me to stand as well. It was a very short moment, but one that I will remember for a very long time, being recognized for my work by this group of respected law-makers.

```
I felt very honored today that I was rec-
ognized for my service in WWII and for our
book that we put out. Today, I felt like I
was really someone! . . . C. Libby
```

We also had the opportunity to stop and watch a press conference that was taking place where many of the top military officers of Pennsylvania were present to honor Gold and Blue Star Mothers. Sgt. Libby stood to the side and listened as he reflected back on the many families that lost loved ones in WWII and the fact that his mother at one time was a Blue Star Mom. One of the top officers came to meet Sgt. Libby and insisted on a photograph and could not wait to order and read the books. A great day full of tribute, honor, respect, recognition and new friendships. Our gratitude goes out to both the representatives for having us there and for all the memories we have from our day at The Capital! Now, racing onward to 101 years old, we hope that the press will continue to be kind and reach out to Sgt. Libby for him to speak and be interviewed while he is still here and able to tell his stories.

A way to educate the masses on these interesting and important topics as well as being able to brag about having not just one, but two books on the market for people to enjoy, Sgt. Libby is still moving full-steam ahead! Knowledge is a powerful tool and education for the future generations is a step that we must all take in contributing to that knowledge. For the right choices and decisions to be made about society's issues will be in the hands of someone else long after we are gone. Leave them with good advice and sage wisdom to reflect on and use for the betterment of our great country.

Life At 100 Years

✳ ✳ ✳

95, 96, 97, 98, 99 and . . . . 100! Close your eyes for a moment and try to comprehend the countdown in life to be able to look at someone and respond to their question of how old you are and from your lips, have the ability to say to them, *"I am 100 years old"*.

Weather reports mention that on October 3, 1917, it was unusually cold. Move the calendar and clocks forward on Sgt. Libby's 100th birthday in 2017, we had a bright sunny day to travel around his hometown and take as many photos as we could capturing that special day and interacting with our usual Q&A session as I prepare this book. A light jacket is all that we would need on this October Pennsylvania day, much different than the conditions his parents faced as the newborn Charles A. Libby entered the world. I commented to him as we walked through downtown Williamsport that The Lord has prepared a wonderful day for your 100th birthday. He would smile and comment that it must had been a gift to him on his special day.

One photo taken of Sgt. Libby by myself that is only explained by his *many* blessings from God captured that perfect moment of the sun shining through the skies as a beam of glorious light perfectly hit Sgt. Libby. As if God was saying *Happy Birthday Charlie*, the rays shot out of the Heavens to warm him as he looked upward to the wonderful present to honor him from The Hudock Capital Group had arranged for him. A large billboard that advertisers can purchase ads featuring their businesses showed two different photos of Sgt.

Libby with a message of gratitude for his service and a Happy 100th Birthday. Drivers honked their horns as they saw the Sgt. himself standing near this display and his own beam of light radiated from his ear-to-ear smile at what he saw that special day in the center of his hometown. Pride and pure joy exploded from his very being the entire trip around town as he was able to *brag* a little on himself that on that day, he turned 100 years old!

Sgt. Libby on his 100th birthday with Rays of
Light surrounding him from Heaven.
Photo 2017 by Steve Hunter.

Turning the clocks back to further add to this story, I first met Sgt. Libby at his 90th birthday party. I was waiting for the big surprise to yell *Happy Birthday* to an old man that would enter the building with either a cane or walker. His arm wrapped around another person's to aid in walking and to be carefully seated at a table to enjoy the many people that would come up to him throughout the evening and yell into his ears due to not being able to hear them. I pictured in my mind a man that was beaten up from the war and attending a party that would be one of his last. The many relatives who gathered to give both their well wishes *and* their final goodbyes was my mind's picture. Well, . . . that was not the case at all! In fact, I was so shocked at what I saw that I still remember my jaw hitting the floor when they told me that *this* was the birthday boy.

He was able to sneak in under the radar and ruined the big surprise, but we all yelled anyhow when all had seen him. I looked over at the door as I heard it open to see a older gentleman coming in at full gallop. I mean, he was walking as fast as any healthy person at 40 years old! He was dressed nicely and had a big smile on his face. When I heard the crowd finally yelling Happy Birthday to him, I had to go to his eldest son Chuck and ask him where his dad was. Chuck laughed and pointed to him. I said, *"That's him? That's your 90 year old dad?"* We both laughed and I promptly introduced myself and wished him a big happy birthday. The entire evening, I watched him in awe as he danced with every woman there, ran around like he owned the joint and enjoyed this party that I soon realized was *not* going to be his last.

What a treat to have this as my first introduction to the man that I would spend so much time with, grow to know and grow to love with all of my heart. It was a few years later when I was asked to listen to his stories and to think about writing his life story into a book, but each time prior to that when I saw him, I was always amazed at his youthfulness. Now, I can say that I have never met another person quite like him and that I have been so blessed to have had these opportunities and learning experiences over these past ten years with him. I make sure at the end of every telephone call, every meeting and every gathering to tell him God bless you and that I love him!

I also enjoy talking to him about random things and off-the-cuff things just to spark a memory and to also get a point of view from a man who has lived so long and seen so many things. In stories we tell together, being a driver of a command car, tanks, jeeps and all types of military vehicles, I asked him about all the other forms of transportation that he has traveled in.

I wrote about his train-jumping antics as a child, so that took care of that form of travel. I then asked him about helicopters and he commented that he's never been on one and didn't ever care to get on one! I followed up with airplanes, which was another topic that we had often discussed in depth previously. When you stop and think about the development of flight, he has seen it all! Predating Sgt. Libby by only 14 years, the first flight and the first flying machines were still fresh and new in our world. He recalls the old black and white reels of planes taking flight and then quickly crashing. He also remembers the comedy of the times in the silent movies and how the failed attempts of flight pioneers made for great entertainment.

```
I've been on a plane only on one occasion.
My wife Ginny and I went to Florida and
back a long time ago. When we took off, she
wondered why he was going up at the steep
angle and when he was going to stop. She was
afraid of how high the pilot was taking us.
I told her, he'll level off in a minute. That
was the one and only time that I have flown.
I have seen many planes, some friendly and
some shooting at me. I really don't know how
they stay up there . . . C. Libby
```

The advancement of flight by taking a man to the moon and back, breaking the speed of sound, the space shuttles and The International Space Station all are remarkable things that have occurred within his lifetime and still amaze him that he has seen such advancement in his 100 years on this earth.

The telephone to cellular phones, Morse code to e-mails, street cars to bullet trains, camp fires to microwaves, outhouses to modern smart rest-rooms, lasers, drones, wireless technology, artificial organs and so many advancements that Sgt. Libby wonders how we came this far when so many people in the world have no absolutely common sense at all.

Recently, I managed to catch him at the right moment and get a gem for the book. This is a 100 year old man in his normal routine which he likes to do each and every day, if he is not dancing with younger women. Sgt. Libby is still still active on the exercise machine a few times each day to stay limber and keep his legs strong. I was amazed and thought it worthy of placing into this chapter since we call this book 100 Years of Stories! If you are looking for the answers to how to stay healthy and live a long life, I guess we should all follow the formula of Sgt. Charles Libby!

Sgt. Libby not giving into age, still active in life! *Photos 2017 by Steve Hunter.*

One thing that I have noticed in my blessed time of friendship with Sgt. Libby is that sometimes there are no filters to what is thought, said or suggested. The gloves come off quite often on delicate matters where he *needs* to make a stern point based upon right or wrong and what he has learned about that certain issue in his 100 years of life. His sons and his daughter will tell you that he has been pretty much like this for the past 50 or 60 years, but they listen in a different manner now since he has reached this milestone age and nearing the end of his days on this place we call planet earth. This section of the book will be dedicated to the opinions, beliefs and sayings that Mr. Libby is famous for among his family and friends. A section where he shares experience with a dose of common sense and a big heaping helping of *in your face!*

Let's start with the fact that he is a fierce Penn State football fan! DO NOT call or bother him during a game. His love for the game and his love for the football program there is that of a true fan. He also watches other sports and enjoys finding the ones that are truly talented and equally enjoys pointing out the bad calls by the refs as well as the players that he calls *hot dogs*.

The 2016 Presidential primaries / election process . . . Campaigns of the many that threw their hats into the ring and then the ultimate showdown between Hillary Clinton and Donald Trump. This election and the vocal opposition to people having their own guns taken away by Hillary prompted Sgt. Libby to take a stand by cleaning his pistol, having it ready at all times, speaking in favor of the NRA and the second amendment rights of US citizens as well as getting his concealed handgun permit at 99 years old! It was my honor to drive him to the sheriff's office and help him in the application procedure. I enjoyed watching as he had his photo taken and was presented with this new card. The woman at the desk could not believe that he was that old and still in that good of shape and mental sharpness. He smiled and told her that he was in the war with General Patton and quickly announced where he was and all the major battles that he was in.

If you haven't ever seen a veteran watch the news and want to reach into the screen and strangle the person talking, you need to put one you know in front of a television that is showing a political race. It is truly entertaining. And as far as the outcome of the latest presidential race, Sgt. Libby is very happy about the outcome!

THE 100 YEAR BIRTHDAY BASH!

All of us at some time or another have had to plan some sort of a gathering, family event or a child's birthday party. Not many of us have the honor of planning a birthday bash for a person known as a *centenarian*, a person turning 100 years old. It was a welcomed endeavor shared by myself, Sgt. Libby's children and Virla Ocker at *The Nippenose Valley Village*. This facilities owners graciously offered to host this big event and we were glad to accept their invitation. Located in the small Pennsylvania community of Oval, it houses veterans and seniors alike who enjoy the peaceful community and the great view of the mountains and farmland from their front porch. It is our hope that they will be as gracious for Sgt. Libby's super-centenarian party when he reaches the new title of a person that is 110 years or older.

I sat at my computer just an hour before I left to make final preparations for this birthday bash and enjoy this big dose of reality that I am faced with. I was about to toast a man that in a matter of nine days would be 100 years old! My excitement and my anxiety were both running high as I prepared what I would say, the events that I would lead everyone through and knowing that I would be meeting several politicians that would come to pay tribute to Sgt. Libby as well.

Upon arrival to this birthday celebration, all of my fears and doubts about how it would go disappeared. Prayer on the trip there calmed me down and it became a welcomed chore to do what I was about to do.

Guests started to arrive, name tags were issued to each indicating whether they were friends or family and music played in the background with the sounds of wartime big band music that I knew would be pleasing to Sgt. Libby upon his arrival.

Up until this day, Sgt. Libby was told that he would be doing a short speech for the residents there at Nippenose Valley Village. As he entered the facility, many started to gather around him with warm greetings and admiration. I could tell by looking across the room that he was not only being gracious, but he was also glancing around the room to catch a glimpse of me.

When he caught my eye and knew he had my attention, he motioned for me to come that way. I walked over to him, hugged him and said softly in his ear, *"Happy Birthday!"* He responded back to me in the way he jokes privately with me in situations like this, *"You piss-pot!"*. I laughed, he laughed and I told him I loved him and that this was all for him and to enjoy the day. Once again, in true Sgt. Libby fashion, he said that he thought he was doing a speech and never realized that anything like this was going on. He smiled and politely said to me thank you and I told him once again that I loved him.

Food was prepared by Chip which was elegant and very appealing to the guests. It was served and the people, with the music still playing, continued to fill the large room. Over 150 guests would arrive to wish him well and see what all would be planned for this special day. I announced on the microphone that we would be starting a formal presentation in ten minutes and guests took their seats anxiously waiting for what we had planned for this 100 year old WWII veteran. Many other veterans were present and some wore their uniforms as a form of honoring Sgt. Libby that special day.

Chairs were arranged in the front of the room for the VIP guests that day as well. As Sgt. Libby was escorted to his special chair, the others started taking their seats and he became very curious as to who all these nicely dressed people were seated close to him.

I began the ceremony by speaking about how we met, how I started the writing of his first book and how he had become a father figure to me. I then surprised him with a framed photo of what this, his new book, would look like and announced to the crowd the name and it was received with applause. I then began to announce the VIP's one-by-one as they each stood at the podium and shared stories, speaking highly of Sgt. Libby. Each VIP awarded him with their specific citations from their respective governmental offices.

The appreciation that poured out really hit Sgt. Libby hard and you could feel that he was truly honored at that moment.

The following special guests and citations were awarded to Sgt. Libby that day. Bonnie Katz, Williamsport City Council presented him with a Certificate of Recognition for his service in WWII. Senator Patrick Toomey of Pennsylvania, *who could not be present*, mailed a certificate which I presented to him for his service with Special Congressional Recognition. Lycoming County Commissioner, Jack McKernan and County Secretary Richard Mirabito also presented him with a Certificate of Recognition for his service in WWII and for his 100 year milestone.

Funny event happened when Vice-chairman of the Lycoming County Commissioners Office came to the facility earlier in the day to give his respects. He didn't realize that Sgt. Libby was still independent and as healthy and spry as he is. He also signed the document presented by their office.

PA House of Representatives member, Representative Jeff Wheeland presented him with a citation and an invitation to come and join him on the House floor for a session to be further honored. Williamsport's Mayor Gabe Campana presented him with a citation and proclaimed that on October 3, 2017, Williamsport would celebrate Mr. Charles Libby Day. This was a very exciting honor for Mr. Libby as he smiled and started planning immediately what he would do on his special day around town. PA Senator Tom Marino also came to honor Sgt. Libby, closing out the presentations with a speech about the old neighborhood, family that served and how his own family has known Sgt. Libby for many years. Congressman Marino awarded him a Certificate of Recognition as well as presenting him with an American Flag and a special pin that he said tongue and cheek, would get Sgt. Libby into the House of Congress and nobody would say a word to him. He didn't waste any time placing that on his uniform when he arrived at his home after the event and still shows it off at functions to others.

From Left to Right : Rick Mirabito, Jack McKernan, Gabe Campana, Sgt. Libby, Tom Marino, Jeff Wheeland, Steve Hunter. *Photo credit 2017 by Angelina Hunter.*

Guests filed out, hands were shaken, hugs were given and many thanks were given all around by many. I thank the group that I had the privilege of working with to make this birthday bash such a success. I look forward to planning the next big milestone of Birthday Bash 105 and wait to see by then what kind of celebrities will come to honor this blessed man.

Sgt. Libby with his various awards presented to him on his 100th birthday.
Photo credit 2017 by Steve Hunter.

A month or so after the big birthday bash, Sgt. Libby was once again honored at an event called *Hometown Heroes*. This organization started by a group affiliated with the local VA, led by George Heiges, Jr., Msgt. US Air Force Retired, developed a program whereas local merchants, businesses and families sponsor a banner that hangs on the street light poles featuring a picture of their chosen veteran. With their name, official ranking and branch of service listed on these full-color banners, these veterans are honored around the entire community each and every day for drivers to see and remember.

Sgt. Libby was sponsored by The Williamsport Crosscutters, a local minor league baseball team. At the ceremony, many local veterans attended including the Korean War Veterans of Lycoming County Honor Guard, presented the flag at the opening of the ceremony. Citizens and family members alike were in attendance as more than 75 veterans were announced and honored with banners with a bell sounding for the ones that were either KIA or have passed on since their days of service. It was a very touching moment of this day's events. A special announcement was made by both George Heiges and PA State Representative Garth Everett for Sgt. Libby as the crowd gave him a big round of applause recognizing his 100th birthday milestone.

```
I was surprised that they announced me at
the ceremony. I thank all of the local vet-
erans and families that recognized me for
my birthday and my time in the second world
war . . . C. Libby
```

Indiantown Gap, PA was an important place in the journey of Sgt. Charles Libby. After joining the 109th, this base would be a temporary home to this young soldier. Many fond stories were told to me in our initial interviews and are captured in both books. One constant thing that had been mentioned to me was the fact that he had not been back there to see the base since his military service in the 1940's.

```
It's been so long since I have been there, I
bet it has changed quite a bit. I wonder if
tent city is still there . . . C. Libby
```

In my research to gather as many interesting stories for readers and to give a WWII veteran some form of closure and enjoyment alike, I prepared a trip to visit this Pennsylvania reserve base. I contacted two friends of mine that I knew would be of help, to not only understand what was there and how to find things, but also needed very knowledgeable people in military affairs.

Barb Spaventa helped us in other events and has a wealth of contacts that always come in handy in such matters. She would also act as an additional photographer for us on this historic visit. Veteran, 1st Sgt. Retired US Army, Denny Bennett, former instructor at the base and later, member of Homeland Security, was put in charge of helping me to find out something even more special to Sgt. Libby. His assignment was not only to be our tour guide for the day, but to help me to locate where Sgt. Libby's first captain and later the commander of the 628th Tank Destroyer Battalion was buried. Sgt. Libby thought that he may have been laid to rest here in PA, but was unsure of where the family had him buried.

```
I  heard  about  the  passing  of  Lt.  Col.
Gallagher well after his funeral. If I'd of
known about it at the time, I would have
been there to see him one last time and to
take part in his funeral services. It both-
ers me to this day and I wish that I could
have been there for him. I would really like
to know where he is buried and to go and
visit his grave to show my respects . . .
C. Libby
```

So, with that in mind, the team went to work and in a successful way! We found that he was not only buried in Pennsylvania, but he was laid to rest at the base in Indiantown Gap! We contacted the museum curator, Charles Oellig, and also made arrangements for a private tour during our visit. Preparations were in place and all that was remaining was for me to tell Sgt. Libby the exciting news.

When I told him that we were going to Indiantown Gap to see the museum and drive around the base, he was very excited. Then I sprung the even more exciting news on him that we had found Lt. Col. Gallagher's gravesite. The shocked look on his face said it all and many emotions filled his very being. The excitement of finally knowing where he was buried and that we would be going there was overwhelming to him to say the least. The sadness of knowing that his friend and the man he respected so greatly was passed has always hit him hard. The sense of responsibility in what he was about to do then took precedent over all other emotions and he began the checklist of what I was to help him with as we prepared for the big day.

I am going to need a dozen yellow flowers to
lay on his grave. I'll wear my uniform and
give him a proper tribute for all he did for
me . . . C. Libby

The day came, we all assembled and it was off to what they simply refer to as *The Gap*. He relived stories the entire way there and the closer we got, the more important this entire event became. As we arrived, the entrance was completely different to him and he asked where we were. We told him that we were here and we stopped to take a few photos of this special place.

It looked entirely different to me, but it
was beautiful! It certainly wasn't like this
when I was there in my 20's . . . C. Libby

We found the information center and were instructed as to how to navigate around the grounds to find the grave-site that we looked for. Denny ran reconnaissance and found the plot that we were looking for. Making our way around the other grave markers and ensuring that Sgt. Libby could make it all the way to the site through the grass, we finally came upon the correct site and the moment that he has waited for since 1992.

As he approached the final resting place of his commanding officer, Sgt. Libby spoke softly as if talking to himself as he looked down at the grave marker. He stood with arms behind his back and we all moved back to give him room as he soaked in this long awaited moment. As sadness started to fill his mind, his hands moved to his face covering his eyes as he began to weep for his longtime friend who he respected so power-fully. I too began to weep as I watched this WWII veteran show and release these bottled up emotions.

Sgt. Libby weeping at the grave site of his commanding officer, Fort Indian Town Gap.
Photo 2017 by Steve Hunter.

He asked for the flowers that we had brought and I handed them to him. He hiked up a pant leg as he balanced himself. He stooped down at the grave marker, laid the beautiful yellow flowers down and reached out his hand, touching the words etched into the stone.

Sgt. Libby paying tribute to his commanding officer. *Photos 2017 by Steve Hunter.*

Right there as if he was holding his own ceremony to honor him, Sgt. Libby spoke of how this man was so special to him and thanked him for what he taught and did for him as a younger man. The moment was powerful and something that I will always remember throughout my entire life. We all hugged and consoled him as Sgt. Bennett and Sgt. Libby both called us to attention as they saluted and then ended the ceremony by a newer tradition of pouring out a beer near the stone as if they had just shared their last drink together. We also had single flowers that the rest of us laid on the grave in respect. Upon conclusion of this private ceremony, Barb took Sgt. Libby's arm and we all quietly walked off the cemetery grounds and got back into the car to move to our next visitation spot at the base.

Several photos were taken by both myself and Barb of this occasion as well as a full video documentation of the event. To mark 25 years of his passing and a closing of a chapter in the mind of this WWII veteran was certainly worth taking the day to drive to The Gap and fulfill a dream of a hero.

I had stated many times within my writings, as I mention Lt. Col. Gallagher's life, his ranking. At the start of young Libby driving him, he was a captain. Upon the tragic death of Col. Hernandez, he took his position, moving up in ranks to assume this spot. We were all amazed and happy to see when we all looked at the grave marker of what we had found. At the time of serving this great country upon retirement, Gallagher was now Major General, two-star! And, not only did he participate in WWII but also served in the Korean War *and* Vietnam! I guess you can see now why Sgt. Libby had such admiration for this great man. He knew his character, his love for country and his ability to lead men into war. What an opportunity to have learned about him and what a blessing to have participated in this small ceremony for another important American Hero! God bless you General Gallagher and may you always rest in peace with The Lord knowing that others appreciated and loved you here.

The trip wasn't over and we still had an appointment to visit the base museum. As we entered, Sgt. Libby's eyes lit up and he immediately started looking and commenting on the items that were close to the door. We were greeted by the museum curator, Charles Oellig with a warm hand shake and smile. As I introduced the group, he indicated that he had been waiting for us and welcomed us to the newly renovated museum. Stories started right away out of the mouth of Sgt. Libby and he was off and running! I was amazed at what they had preserved and enjoyed listening to the many stories they both shared. Charles is a wealth of information as to the base history and himself is a retired soldier.

We presented him with a copy of *From The Command Car* and we were presented with a book on the history of the base. Sgt. Libby then pulled out a copy of the *Letter of Protection* to present to our new friend. He explained the letter and how he carried it during WWII. The curator then mentioned that within the archives of the base, they had several letters that they had preserved from soldiers writing home that dated back to the Civil War and maybe even earlier. He said that he had seen a few that had something very similar. I asked him if he could find a history on this particular one or something that was near to it and he agreed that in his free time that he would try to locate some of them.

About three weeks later he delivered and I received many different copies of letters and information that was very similar to the letter that Sgt. Libby carried. It is no surprise that other believers in God had carried similar letters. We were both very excited to see such letters and equally excited that his will now also be a part of that same history to share with future generations. Many people now carry it and many soldiers that are currently deployed also carry it as a form of inspiration and protection in their dangerous daily duties.

We all got hungry after driving the post and looking at vintage preserved fighter planes, tanks and other military vehicles, so we went to a local restaurant that is frequented by many of the soldiers stationed there. We all entered and Sgt. Libby was quick to approach tables and shake the hands of the men in uniform. They all noticed the hat he wears and knew that it meant WWII and were all happy to shake his hand and thank him for his service. We had our meal and were informed by the waitress that our bill had been paid for by a table of soldiers. We thanked her and were then approached by several of the men coming to say thank you and to shake his hand. You could tell that he was honored and that he felt the celebrity status that day. As the many soldiers left the restaurant, I commented to Sgt. Libby that we should hang out longer because dinner would only be a few hours away and it may mean another free meal. He smiled and chuckled and said, *no we better get to our next stop.*

We drove to the base PX and went inside to see what we could find. Lining the walls and filling the many shelves and racks were military needs such as patches, insignia, shirts, pants and any other items the soldiers may need there on the base or for when they deploy to their location of combat. Sgt. Libby gazed at all the items and enjoyed seeing the young soldiers preparing for what they were in store for. We spoke to many and they enjoyed shaking his hand as well as accepting the Letter of Protection he offered each and every one of them. I enjoyed a question from one of the sergeants that was there listening to a story he was telling, *"What does that T mean on his sleeve?"* I told him about the old ranking of TEC Sgt. and what that entailed. Many hands were shaken, many prayers said for the departing soldiers and off we were again to our next location.

The Bloomsburg Fair was celebrating their 162nd year and featured many buildings of displays, carnival rides and many food vendors. A display of an authentic *Stuie Tank* was also a feature of the fair which had been purchased from a private dealer in England and returned to the Berwick area where it had been built so many years ago for the war effort.

Jack Craft of the Endless Mountains War Museum, several fair officials and veterans of many different military operations were on hand to speak to the public as they filed into one of the buildings. Each year, these veterans gather and take their time to sit each day for almost two weeks to educate people on the topics they are experienced in. Representatives from WWII, Korea, Vietnam, Desert Storm, Afghanistan and many more were on hand for this event. Sgt. Libby was asked to have a seat with all of them and the fun ensued. In true Sgt. Libby fashion, as the oldest member of this panel of veterans, took over and instantly drew a crowd. The time flew by and before we knew it, it was time to get back to our neck of the woods and get this 100 year old vet home to take off his shoes and military uniform and kick his feet up in front of the television and take a nap.

What a day and experience that I had the chance to be a part of! You know that The Lord places people in your path and sometimes deeper within your routine. He allows you to meet people that add value to your own life and provides ways of teaching through their experiences. This is what I am blessed with each and every day that I spend with these great men and women. Thank you Lord!

THE 242ND MARINE CORP BIRTHDAY BASH . . .
The call came in requesting for Sgt. Libby and myself to attend and be the featured guests by the Susquehanna Valley Detachment 308 Marine Corp League in Selinsgrove, PA. We were glad to be a part of such a great organization's celebration and looked forward to the night. Retired Marine and the detachment Commandant, Frank Passaniti, made the call from the Williamsport VA Office and provided us with the details of the evening.

The night was not only based around the birthday anniversary of The US Marine Corp, but was also based upon their many rich traditions that they carry on to this day when celebrating this event. The cake was cut with a Marine parade saber and the first piece was offered to Sgt. Libby as their honored guest. Another was offered to the eldest Marine in the room as was a piece to the youngest.

I was introduced and I began to lighten up the room with some funny stories and had to mention how fitting it was for the US Marines to call in the US Army to speak to them at their birthday. The room was filled with laughter and was followed by a few comments that only a Marine would say while joking with an old GI from the US Army.

Sgt. Libby took the floor and every eye was on him as they enjoyed his stories, applauded at many touching remarks and gave him a standing ovation at the end of our presentation. It was a special evening and we were both proud to be a part of it.

```
They were really a bunch of nice people. I
can't believe that they asked me, a GI, to
come and talk! I guess they liked my stories
that I told them . . . C. Libby
```

ALLENWOOD PRISON GUARDS VETERANS DAY CELEBRATION . . .
Master Sgt. Kevin Bittenbender once again invited us to speak for the guards at the prison he works at. A large group of guards there sat and enjoyed our talk and lined up for Sgt. Libby's first book. Stories to set the tone about WWII and how similar each day spent in a dangerous job compares to theirs by putting their lives on the line. Many veterans and current serving soldiers alike were present to make this day even ore special.

A special plaque was awarded to Sgt. Libby for his service and once again, he enjoyed himself very much.

```
I really enjoyed all of those guards. They
all looked very professional and were really
nice people. The plaque they gave me is very
nice . . . C. Libby
```

100, 101, 102, 103, 104, 105 . . . How many more will there be? As Sgt. Libby often remarks,

"It's up to the good Lord as to how long he keeps me around." But for now, life at 100 seems to be pretty rewarding for this former command car driver, father of three, grandfather of four and great- grandfather of three. The books have given him a new sense of pride and a new life mission to spread his experiences to others within his stories in hopes of helping others to learn from his long and blessed life. As far as the upcoming years, I am sure that I will continue to hear more stories that should have made it into this book. So, keep posted to our website www.fromthecommandcar.com, his Facebook page From The Command Car and look for his many speeches and book signings to hear even more about Sgt. Libby.

Dancing Til The End

✳ ✳ ✳

THE MANY QUESTIONS WHICH I have heard from the hundreds of people that have attended our speeches and book signings of what has kept this man so young are a common occurrence. Questions like, What do you eat? What do you drink? Are you a religious man? What keeps you so young? All of them answered a little differently, but all include the fact that Mr. Libby contributes his mobility, spring in his step and excitement for each day to his long history of dancing. *Yes, dancing!*

It began prior to his enlistment in the CCC Camps and continued there with the other boys. In an effort at a young age to not only fit in but also to meet young ladies, Charles quickly took to the many different dances of the times and adapted them to the era's big band music along with the many singers that he would hear on the family radio.

Some of the songs that Sgt. Libby both enjoys listening and dancing to include *Stardust, Wonderful Tonight, Paper Doll, The Anniversary Waltz, Sincerely, After The Loving, Unforgettable, Moonlight Serenade* and *New York, New York*. Some older, some newer, but the style of the songs allow him to do many types of steps that he learned so many years ago. Another that he enjoys listening to and mimics the movements of Al Jolson himself is *Toot Toot Tootsie, Good-bye*. An old tune from 1927 that still brings him enjoyment and fond memories of the music from his youth.

That Al Jolson was a great singer and
performer. I really enjoy listening to
him! . . . C. Libby

Earlene Martinez was one of the first partners that he remembers dancing with who offered him tips on dancing from her days spent in Chicago
dancing at both *The Aragon* and *Trianon Ballroom*. Their dancing relationship
turned into a romantic relationship right up to the time of entering the service. After returning to the US from serving in the war, there were many
Italian girls that he fondly remembers dancing with at various clubs and ball-
rooms around town. This was a regular activity that his mother encouraged
due to his love of dancing and his skill level.

A young Sgt. Libby with early dance partner and love, Earlene Martinez.
Photos circa 1946, photographer unknown.

Today the names still fly around in the stories of his favorite dance partners like Connie, Nancy, Beverly and Diane as being his favorites to dance with each week to the band of his great friend Cathy. The smile on the face of Sgt. Libby while telling these stories shows his enthusiasm for dancing and getting the attention of these lovely ladies he dances with regularity. Even my own mother, Toni Hunter and my wife Alma had a few chances to dance with Sgt. Libby at a local American Legion Post and other places. My mother commented to me that he danced very smoothly, much like my grandfather also did. Sgt. Libby also commented to me of how well both danced and hoped he would get another chance to dance someday with each of them again.

When talking to Sgt. Libby about dancing long ago, he fondly remembers that he once danced in an airplane hanger at a camp in Fort Worth, Texas. An unusual place to dance, but it worked just fine for the soldiers of his unit when invited by the officials at Camp Bowie.

```
They had called us at Camp Hood, Texas and
wanted to know if we all would come to a
dance they were having in Fort Worth. When
the weekend came, we all went there. When
we got there, it was filled with girls! Some
soldiers and some civilians, they were ev-
erywhere! Some were WAVES, WACS and SPARS
which were military gals. A military band
played all the good stuff that I liked. We
all hated to leave because they treated us
so kindly while we were there. It is a time
that I remember very well and one of the
largest and strangest places that I ever got
to dance . . . C. Libby
```

Another dancing memory that Sgt. Libby is fond of is the time he had to drive and deliver a 6x6 military vehicle to Morris Army Airfield in

Hartsville, NC. Sgt. Libby told me that he had never driven a 6x6 before, but they quickly gave him a tutorial on driving the vehicle and he was ready to fill in for the missing soldier from the motor pool that was unable to make the trip.

He met two older ladies there that invited him and another soldier to stay with them while there. As they spoke about his love for dancing, they became excited and told him about a dance contest that would be happening while he was there. The young Libby had no problem registering for this contest that offered prizes as well as a time to show off and meet some new young ladies.

```
One of the elderly women told me to go and
ask a girl that was standing off to the
side to enter the contest with me. They told
me that they had seen her dance before and
that she was pretty good and we may stand
a chance to win first prize . . . C. Libby
```

The young girl was going to a school there in Hartsville and would soon be graduating. The young and bold Libby approached this pretty girl and asked if she would have a word with him. She gladly accepted and they began to talk.

```
I apologized for interrupting her conversa-
tion with her friends and told her about the
ladies that I was staying with and how they
said she would be a great partner to have in
the upcoming contest they were holding at
12 noon. She said that she would be honored
to dance in the contest with such a handsome
man. She asked me how old I was and I danced
around that and made her guess from 23  28.
```

She laughed and told me again how handsome
I was. I told her that we would have to warm
up with a few dances to get ready for the
contest and she was more than ready to get
started . . . C. Libby

Later that night the contest began with approximately 25 different couples registered. When the contest was over, the judges had the task of choosing the winners from all of these great dancers.

They announced that a man in uniform that was
visiting had won second prize and then they
said my name. The girl and I, which I think
was named Helen, walked to the front while
the crowd clapped and received our prizes. I
can't remember what they gave her, but I got
a really nice pocketbook (wallet). I took it
with me to Europe and remember that I had
$15 in it. I had to leave it in my gear bag
in an old church. The Germans came through
the church while we were in a battle and they
ransacked all of our stuff. They used their
bayonets to cut open all of our bags and took
all of our goodies. I had a medal that was
given to me by a man over there that he got
in WWI and it was in that bag as well. They
got it all and I am still upset that they got
that medal and my wallet . . . C. Libby

After Charles left North Carolina, the two ladies called his mother back in Pennsylvania. Charles had given them his number to stay in touch because they were so nice to him. They told his mother that he was a fine boy and that she was blessed to have him as a son. They also mentioned that he was quite the dancer and told her of his second place results of the dance contest. His mother responded with gratitude and agreed that he was a very good dancer and that he liked to show off a little bit.

A fond memory for Sgt. Libby and a boost of confidence in his love for the activity. His love today for dancing is still as strong and his showing off is equally as brazen. Spinning and twirling his partners on the floor, taking a couple steps with them and dancing them right off of the dance floor are signature moves for this 100 year old dancer. There seems to be no end in sight for his days of enjoying stepping onto the dance floor.

```
My buddy George Hauke used to say to the
other guys at the bar when I would go danc-
ing that if I dressed in a suit and tie, I
was looking for a girl to take home and if
I was dressed in just casual nice clothes, I
would drink beer with all of them. You know
what, he was right . . . C. Libby
```

Sgt. Libby and his wife Virginia also had plenty of fun dancing at the many clubs and events around his hometown. They also enjoyed the activity at the reunions with his fellow soldiers. Until her death in 1997 they even danced in contests at The Moose Club dancing for band leader, musician and lifelong friend Sammy Ray to the Anniversary Waltz. Mr. Libby's mother was even present at this particular event where he asked her if she would dance with him. Sgt. Libby still looks fondly upon that day that he was able to dance with his loving mother and honor her wishes to dance. That was a special moment for Sgt. Libby and his mother and the entire crowd applauded after this special dance.

```
My wife was a pretty good dancer. She said
that I stood out in the crowd. I showed her
a lot of what I knew and we always got the
```

```
looks from other dancers on the dance floor.
Many women who I dance with now ask me why
I don't get a girlfriend or why I don't re-
marry and I tell them all, I'm having too
much fun dancing with whoever I want to and
don't want to be tied down to one gal . . .
C. Libby
```

Recently, Sgt. Libby and I were scheduled for an event at The Union County Library in Lewisburg, Pennsylvania to speak to a group of people about his experiences. As we sat alone waiting for the people to arrive, the topic of dancing came up. In a brief moment, Sgt. Libby gazed off into a memory of dancing with one of his past loves and started singing the lyrics to the song *Stardust*. He took his time, he knew all the words and he smiled as he relived a fond memory of a dance long ago. I listened and watched the love in his face as he recited the lovely words of the song by the late Glenn Miller and his Orchestra . . .

And now the purple dusk of twilight time, steals across the meadows of my heart. High up in the sky the little stars climb, always reminding me that we're apart. You wander down the lane and far away, leaving me a song that will not die. Love is now the stardust of yesterday, the music of the years gone by. Sometimes I wonder why I spend the lonely night dreaming of a song. The melody haunts my reverie and I am once again with you. When our love was new and each kiss an inspiration. But that was long ago, now my consolation is in the stardust of a song. Beside a garden wall when stars are bright, you are in my arms. The nightingale tells his fairy tale, a paradise where roses bloom. Though I dream in vain, in my heart it will remain . . . My stardust melody. The memory of love's refrain.

He finished his song and looked at me and simply said, "*I love that song.*" I could tell that it plays a special part of his memories. Still a sharp mind at 100 and the memories of days gone by are one of the things that lift his spirits up each day as he realizes how many of his fellow C-company buddies he has outlived, how many loves he has lost and how many partners he has led on the many dance floors in his long and blessed lifetime.

If there is music playing, he is always ready to dance. But, now let's see how many requests we get now for him to sing Stardust at future presentations.

In 2017 at the wedding of his eldest son Chuck and new wide Marilyn, it didn't take too long for Sgt. Libby to help get the dancing started when the music caught his ear. He made his approach to where I was and told me that he wanted to dance with my wife Alma. She always enjoys it and feels honored that he chooses her and quickly got up from her seat and the two graced the dance floor dancing to the soft music of Glen Miller. She gets a little nervous at times making sure that she doesn't step on his feet, but Sgt. Libby always makes any woman he dances with comfortable while leading her and whispering tips of which way he will go next.

I enjoyed watching him during the many slow dances and even had the chance to see this 99 year old man dance to some 70's rock and roll like he owned the floor. There wasn't a face there that wasn't smiling and enjoying the show that he put on that day for all to remember for years to come.

I wear many hats in my life and enjoy the creative outlet of writing and am blessed to have someone like Sgt. Libby to feed that passion. But, professionally, I both entertain and spread the word of Jesus to many people. One of the aspects of my ministry is my family act. The Hunter Family Music & Ministry show travels to the many nursing homes, assisted living facilities and hospitals around the state of Pennsylvania and sings the music that many elderly people remember from their earlier years in life.

On many occasions, I have taken Sgt. Libby with us to not only tell a few stories, but to dance with the ladies within these homes. I would feel it safe to say, that when I bring him along, he steals the show! At first, people are shocked to find out how old he is, then he politely asks during the music if a lady would like to dance. He carefully holds them, leads them around the room and escorts each one of them back to their seats as if he was a professional dancer on a cruise ship or at a large hotel or casino. If he wished to do so, I could see him taking on an entirely new career in that line of business.

```
I always treat a lady with courtesy and am
very polite. My mother taught me long ago to
treat them with respect and when I dance, I
am always a gentleman . . . C. Libby
```

Upon returning to the nursing home on our next visit, the many ladies are disappointed if I don't have him with us that day. Again and again, people ask when he will be returning to speak and dance with all of them. A blessing to all and a time for him to share his love and passion with others who appreciate the same type of music as well as sharing his stories of the CCC Camps and his experiences in WWII.

```
I'll do it until the good Lord says that it's
time for him to take me. Until then, I'll
keep having fun and show off for all the
ladies . . . C. Libby
```

Regrets & Blessings In Life

* * *

"In life, there are no do-overs, so make the right choices and you will have little to no regrets."

"You can only live life forward and not in reverse." These among many other sayings ring in the ears of those who contemplate life itself and the path they have traveled, experiencing life's many ups and downs.

Regret is properly defined as such . . . *To look back upon with a feeling of distress or loss or to feel emotional distress of the mind recalling an event.*

As you try your best to imagine, to live 100 years, you are bound to have made some errors in judgment and have some regrets. This section is a few of the things that Sgt. Libby recalls as being regretful and chalks them up into the mistake column.

"Education counts!" . . . His advice to the many of people that think that they know it all and don't need to continue with school. To the young boys and girls that defy their parents and their lack of understanding of what life throws at you in your adult years, heed his words and follow the lead of the ones that made their own mistakes long before you were even born. Trust others who give you advice, not out of greed, but from their hearts to try and save you unpleasant events within your long life you have ahead of you.

```
Don't do it! Stay in school and pursue extra
education far past what is just required of
you and you will stand a better chance in
life in all that you do. I had to quit early
in life and regret it to this day. I missed a
lot of great opportunities because I wasn't
smart enough and couldn't do the job they
needed me to do. Study, work hard and be
successful! Listen to me and listen to your
parents and work hard! . . . C. Libby
```

Sgt. Libby remembers the *lost opportunities* to advance within the military over many occasions that he had to either refuse or wasn't able due to his limited education. Hardship, family need and a little stubborn streak all contributed to leaving school far too early and he regrets it still to this day with great sadness. Education was harder to receive in those days and times, but today, it is right in front of you in many ways and many sources. Strive to perfect your mind, your body and your inner spirit to be successful on your journey through life.

"Tell those you love or care about how you feel!" Sgt. Libby recalls that he wanted to tell his father that he loved him and how much he appreciated all he did for his family, but did not get the chance to before he took his final dying breath in his hospital bed. This floods his mind with the sad memories of his father's passing and even at his advanced age, brings sobbing tears to his clouded eyes.

He also wishes that he could have told his wife of many years before her passing how much he did love her and appreciate what she did for him and his children. All to a memory that can not be forgotten and replays within his mind every day. He wishes that he would have been more attentive and less focused on his work while she was here and living.

His advice to all of the readers of his book is to swallow your pride, don't wait and tell those you love how you feel *before* it is too late. You never know just how long you will have to live with the guilt and the sadness of having *not* done it while you had the chance. Now, at 100 years old, that has been a heavy weight to carry for such a very long time.

Buchenwald concentration camp . . .

```
I wished I had gone to help out and see
the concentration camps and that I still
had the photos that the other GI's gave to
me of the camp to show everyone just what
they did. All the high brass were there at
that time and I missed out meeting all of
them . . . C. Libby
```

Buchenwald held Jews and other POW's that were freed by the US forces. The men of the 628th were asked if they would like to volunteer to go and see the camp and to help with the starving, diseased, injured and dead prisoners. The young driver Libby opted out of this side-mission for personal reasons. He knew what he would see and could not bear to see all of that suffering at that time.

```
After I heard that they were putting all of
them into ovens, I knew it would smell and
I just didn't want to see the children and
the other dead and all of the horror that
everyone was about to see. When the guys got
back, they told me, Charlie, you were right.
It did stink really bad and it was a hor-
rible thing to see . . . C. Libby
```

Some of the guys that did go took photos to document the terrible things that they saw. Some were actually asked to do so for the records of their unit to provide to the courts during the war crimes trials that they knew were going to happen after the war was over. Some of the photos were given to Sgt. Libby at the time that he had preserved within his albums documenting the war. His wife had asked him to throw them away because they were so graphic and after consideration and arguing back and forth, he did so. Now years later that we have been working on the books, he wishes that some of the photos that he had could have been properly preserved within one of his books for all to see.

```
Some people in the world still don't be-
lieve that there were such places. I didn't
go into the camp, but I was there, close by
with my outfit and KNOW that it happened and
that the Nazi's and Hitler were evil mon-
sters! . . . C. Libby
```

Here are two paragraphs of From The Command Car that describe just what they saw . . .

Survivors were like walking skeletons with just skin covering their bones. Some were so weak from malnutrition that they had to be loaded onto stretchers to be taken out of the camp. Others weren't so lucky and died right there in front of our guys before they could be helped. Bodies of Jews lined the camp and were treated by the Germans like trophies or symbols of their might and power. The thought that they were inferior to the Germans gave them a guilt-free attempt to cleanse their country of this race of beloved people.

Upon arrival at the camp, the soldiers who entered it's gates read a sign that hung over the entryway which read *"Jedam das Seine."* The literal German translation of this slogan or saying was *"to each his own."* The slang version of this horrible saying translated as *"everyone gets what he deserves."* This said it all!

This is why people like Sgt. Charles A. Libby went to war and all the others who sacrificed their time and many, their lives. Death came in many forms but this was the type of death that to this day is still completely unbelievable to all mankind. God rest all that suffered and died there and may they rest in peace forever in his kingdom!

Not meeting General Patton is something that he regrets never doing . . .

```
I remember clearly like it was just yes-
terday seeing him from a distance, moving
around talking to our troops, pacing back
and forth. We were ahead of him a little bit
and we all knew at the time that it was him.
I thought to myself he's out here getting
the job done! We were all moving closer to
Germany and we had to move on. There was
no time to try to leave my vehicle and meet
him or even speak to him. We had to move
down another road apart from him to do our
jobs and then his driver took him off in
his jeep. It was a treat getting to see him,
even from a distance . . . C. Libby
```

When asking Sgt. Libby about what he would have said due to his admiration of General Patton, he remembers that he didn't like others in his unit bad-mouthing the general and would have told him the following . . . *You're doing a great job General. We all think that you are getting the job done right!"*

The intensity as I listen to him speak about the man they all called *old blood and guts* is still as fierce and strong as it must have been while serving under the great military leader. I listen to his stories about his admiration of Patton and in the back of my mind, I can't help but wish of the meeting that may have been if the 628th wasn't in the heat of battle between the great general and the hard- working command car driver. Still today, he carries a photo of Patton to speeches and presentations to show his admiration for his military hero and shares historical stories for others to listen to and gain appreciation for his leadership of our American soldiers.

Carbine rifle leaning in my vehicle and not in my hands . . . Many stories I wrote about the war career of Sgt. Libby contained in *From The Command Car* are still told to me regularly and still either bring him great joy or upset him when he thinks about how it could have been different. One such story he would like to slip into the regrets category of this manuscript.

His vehicle needed to be overhauled and he had taken it back to the rear echelon for repairs. He was to spend some time there while they finished and then come back to the front with the repaired vehicle. *Read the full story from his first book From The Command Car.*

As the command car driver, Charles was in charge of making sure that his vehicle ran without any types of mechanical problems. Along the path toward Bergstein, Germany, Charles had noticed that the engine was starting to miss and wasn't firing on all cylinders. Captain Jones instructed Charles to take the vehicle back to ordinance to have a new engine placed in this valuable transport vehicle. He told Charles that he would probably be there for at least three days and to wait there with the command car until the job was completed.

The first night in ordinance, Charles bedded down near his vehicle where it was staged for the mechanics of the unit to change the engine out on the very next morning. As Charles was resting and getting himself prepared for the night's sleep, he heard a noise coming from the hedgerow near him and stayed motionless. An officer from the unit tugged at his foot in an attempt to tell him that there were Germans in the camp.

```
I actually heard both of them laughing, the
Germans. One was standing on the roots of the
hedges and the other was below him holding
```

him up. The officer whispered, there's Krauts in here. My carbine was still in the truck. I hadn't gotten it out yet. I usually keep right beside me every night in case I get ambushed during my sleep. I couldn't believe that they were laughing and being so loud. The American officer shot his .45 through the hedges at the two German soldiers. They disappeared and fired a burp gun right back at us through the thick hedges. This was one of the few times that I got really scared. I hid under the front wheel of the command car for cover. I could hear the bullets zipping through the grass past me from the German burp gun. I wished that I would have had my gun close to me at the time. I really wasn't sure how many of them there were. The other officer that fired the pistol just rolled over and went to sleep like it wasn't anything big. Before I had crawled back into my fart-sack, I made sure that I had my gun beside me and that it was ready to fire if there was a next time! No other problems the rest of the night, thank God . . . C. Libby

He has commented to me that he's not sure what would have happened that night if he had his rifle, but one thing is for sure, he would have been better prepared and able to help out that officer if the weapon was at the ready. He is grateful that they fled after the pistol was shot toward them, but the memory still haunts him that he was unprepared to fight back that night.

Halting of the 628th reunions . . . Reunions for this great tank unit were a highlight of Sgt. Libby's life after returning to the states. Getting a stable job and starting his family became the priority in his young life. Gatherings of these brave soldiers took them to many different cities throughout the years to share old stories and new stories alike.

> Gallagher and many of the guys from the outfit would come to these reunions. My wife and I would go and have a great time sharing stories and laughing with all of them. One reunion, my buddy Kranz asked me how my arms were that I burned. I rolled up my sleeves and showed him how they healed and he was really surprised that they healed so good. He remembered how bad they were just before I was to ship back home. He told me, Charlie, I'm glad they healed up so well. We all cared about each other and I guess I wasn't the only one that remembered stuff about the war . . . C. Libby

The final reunion between soldiers of this unit was held in Fredericksburg, Virginia sometime in the early to middle 1990's at The Eisenhower Inn. The date is a little fuzzy to Sgt. Libby, but the feeling of that last one is still very clearly felt today. This regret is not trying to keep the reunions going until there were no more tank men to attend.

> When we started the reunions, 224 of us came but at this one there were only 14 of us attended. It was nice to see the other 14 fellas, but sad that so many could not attend or were already dead. At the end of the reunion, someone called for a vote to see whether or not we should continue the reunions or close them up. Everyone there

```
voted to stop them because it would be too
hard for us at our age to keep them going.
I still think about how many of my fellow
soldiers are alive and how much I would like
to talk to them and see how they look . . .
C. Libby
```

At this final reunion, Mr. Libby also found out that the man who led their unit into battle and the first officer that he drove, Lt. Col. William J. Gallagher, had passed away. His regret is that he was not able to be there to be a part of the funeral and celebration of his life for all he did for him as a young driver and for what he did for The United States of America!

```
If I would have known that he had passed away,
I would have been there for sure. I respected
him very much and he was a great leader to
all of us boys. I wished that I would have
kept in closer touch with him but with a fam-
ily and a garbage route, it was hard to do. I
still miss him to this day . . . C. Libby
```

As an interviewer, I could see in the telling of this particular story that he wishes he would have voted the other way. His need for contact with these brave boys he served with lies deep within his daily routines. His need for closure as each of his buddies are known to have passed on is another yearning thought within his mind each night as he closes his eyes to go to sleep, wondering if he will be the next soldier to be laid to rest. Whether they were Italian, Jewish, Polish or German, they were all his brothers-in-arms and they still mean the world to him.

I sense a responsibility within his very soul that he may or may not be the final living soldier of the men who fought throughout the heart of the war, were there to receive the Victory Medal and that have the ability to claim they were members of the 628th Tank Destroyer Battalion and members of what was known as "C" Company.

As the author and close friend and somewhat of an adopted son of this WWII hero, I am trying to piece together the information that haunts him each and every day. Researching obituaries and military records, calling people who may know something, tracking down relatives and meeting people that were in someway associated with these great men to get this answer . . . *Is he the last one?* I hope that the question can be answered soon. Either a meeting between some of the final members of this great unit or a feeling of closure in his mind that his brothers are all resting and safe in the arms of The Lord.

Blessings are defined as such . . . *Anything that gives happiness or prosperity.*

Just as you can imagine that there may have been a few regrets in the life of a man that has lived for a century, you can also picture in your mind the many blessings that he has received by living the life of service that he has lived. This section will address things that he has claimed were or still are blessings within his life.

Getting to know his grandmother as a child . . . Mrs. Ida Libby, *Grammie* to the young Charles Libby. A stern woman, but full of love for her family. A mother of 11 children says it all! Sgt. Libby remembers some of the times he spent at her house in Weichart, PA.

```
If I would go to the cookie jar, she would
tell me, NO cookies before dinner. You'll
ruin your dinner! I told her that I was
just looking to see what kind she had in
the jar and she told me that if I ate all
of my dinner that I could have one after or
maybe even two. I also remember that if I
```

```
pouted or looked sad, she'd tell me to turn
that lip up where it belongs. She would bake
bread and cooked for everyone. I'll tell ya,
when she cooked, it was really good . . .
C. Libby
```

A moment of reflecting back to a childhood that was so long ago. A love for a woman that has been gone for many years and brings back so many pleasant memories to him.

Coming home from the war alive . . . Many of his fellow soldiers did not make it home alive and many of them died from their injuries later. Sgt. Libby states it simply on this topic of how he felt then and how he feels still to this very day . . .

```
I am glad that I came home alive and the
good Lord was with me all the time and with-
out him, I would have surely been killed.
It almost happened many times, but I always
came out of it okay . . . C. Libby
```

My late wife Virginia (Ginny) . . . I was at a dance and she, my wife, was there and I met her in passing but didn't pay too much attention at first. She had a big family including six sisters and they all were good looking and nice ladies. He remembers that he didn't dance with her at first but thought she had a nice figure and wanted to very soon. Charles was a worker on the assembly line at a company called Ray-O-Vac, where they made batteries and Virginia worked there as well. One day he asked her if she danced and told her that he would like to dance with her at the Moose Club the next time he saw her there. She agreed and the next time they were both there, they did have that dance. One dance led to another and after about a two year romance, they became married and quickly started their family together.

That family that they started over 65 years ago is his source of joy and blessings in life to this day. He may not have done it all correctly along the way, but the good Lord saw fit to have placed her in his life to give him what he needed later in life and for this she truly blessed him.

My children . . . Sgt. Libby has been blessed with three wonderful children that all live either with him or near him. He is very proud of the people that they have become and can't say enough good things about them to others. They are all grounded in life through their belief in God and his son Jesus Christ. They are all walking testaments of his living word and take every opportunity to show others his love in their ability to comfort, help and be there for others at any time.

They are all a true blessing in life of Sgt. Libby and to have his family near him each and every day is a very special thing to him. You can still see the father correcting and making sure that they are all alright in his words to them as if he still needs to protect and take care of their every need even while they are taking care of his needs in his advanced age. It is truly a wonderful thing to see and witness and he has mentioned this blessing many times over to me throughout our friendship and these interviews.

Family is important to him and throughout all that you read about this man, you can tell that he values this more than anything in his life. A true blessing and a great example of what God intends for us in this lifetime.

My books . . . Sgt. Libby has expressed that his mother and father would be proud of him for the success of his book *From The Command Car.* He also can't believe that I found enough information and stories to write and publish a second one about him. He is proud to have this accomplishment and finds this blessing something that keeps him motivated each and every day.

Not going to school for very long in his youth also is a source of sadness that somehow brings a mental band-aid to him. Libraries want him to speak there, high schools have had him do presentations for the kids, the book is in both public and school libraries which all is a sort of closure for him. You can see the pride in his face as he holds a copy and asks the person hearing the story if they know who he looked like on the cover when he was only 23 years of age. To hear him explain where they can purchase a copy for their own and that everything within the pages is the truth! It surely is a special thing to witness.

Guardian angles and being blessed . . . There are so many stories that just amaze me of this man's toughness, his spark and his love for having an exciting life. I often ask him if he thinks that he is blessed or has guardian angels watching over him.

```
I have been told by many that I am blessed and
when I ask them why, they tell me that I must
have done something that someone up above no-
ticed. I hope I have guardian angels watching
over me, it does seem like it . . . C. Libby
```

He never seems to amaze me in regards to having so many stories to share during my many interviews. One such story came from looking through old photos and further proof of his protection from above was revealed once again while looking at a photo of a tree stand 20 feet in the air at his family hunting camp in northern Pennsylvania.

```
I climbed up to the top step and reached up
to grab a railing that was there. The rail-
ing came loose and came off of the stand. At
that moment, I knew I was going down! I went
backwards off of the steps and I though to
myself, this is it! I hit the ground on my
back and hit really hard. I caught my breath
and I whistled for my son Chuck. Right away
```

```
I heard him say to another guy, Dad fell off
the stand. They both came over and carried
me out of the woods and took me to the hospi-
tal. I was lucky that I didn't hit my head. I
hurt my back and my ankle, other than that,
I was just sore and had to walk with a crutch
for a little while . . . C. Libby
```

The doctors at the hospital looked Sgt. Libby over and were amazed that he was not only alive but that he didn't really have anything wrong with him except a sprained ankle. If this is not proof of having a guardian angel lift him and set him down on the ground, I don't know what is!

The time that he spent relaxing to get over the soreness he was watching television and remembers seeing the coverage of terrorist cowards flying planes into the twin towers. So, in doing the math, he was 83 years old at the time of the injury. WOW!

So, I asked him after hearing the amazing story of his fall about seeing the planes hit the towers in New York City and he responded as such . . .

```
That son of a b! When I saw it, I thought to
myself I hope they get him. I also thought
that I'd like to be there to help get him.
I saw that woman jump out of the building
and thought, oh my God, she'll never make it.
A big ball of fire and a terrible thing to
see and was pert near crying to see it . . .
C. Libby
```

Obviously, speaking of Bin Laden, he was angered by what he saw and the mindset of a military veteran is that he was ready to put the uniform back on and get busy!

So, in regards to the blessings of Sgt. Libby, he feels that telling all of these stories is not bragging, but sharing his life with others is something that he feels is important.

```
I've lived this long, I'm going to keep tell-
ing them to the ones who will listen. I pray
at night to God and Jesus that I am forgiven
for anything I did that did not please him
and that he will have me in that special
place when I finally pass on . . . C. Libby
```

I know that I am blessed to be able to listen, capture them and share them with many more people than he can ever talk to in his daily routine. Enjoy them, learn from them and be blessed yourselves. And, count you many blessings and live a life with as few regrets as you can.

Soldiers, Families and Stories Shared

✳ ✳ ✳

WHAT A PRIVILEGE IT HAS been to travel around with Sgt. Libby to the many functions that not only have honored him for his service to our great country, but also to many others that we have both had the honor of meeting. While speaking with him and becoming friends over these past few years since the release of *From The Command Car*, I have listened to many stories along with the crowds and it has been a source of great inspiration. Through the many tears I have shed as I saw the heart-filled expression of loss, hardships and tragedy while the many US veterans share their stories of war and of life itself, it has been a priceless experience for me. I feel a true connection to each and every one of them.

Here are some of the more notable experiences that I chose to share with readers of these serviceman, families, patriots and heroes we have interacted with in our shared journeys.

CHARLES MISSIGMAN . . .

We spoke of this man in *From The Command Car*. He was one of the first veterans that I had the pleasure to meet along with Sgt. Libby and listen to their shared and intense discussions about WWII. An entire chapter entitled *Two WWII Veterans Meet*, is included in *From The Command Car*. What a remarkable man that I wished I would have had time to write his story! God Bless you Mr. Missigman and RIP with all the other heroes of this Greatest Generation!

JOHN ESPOSITO, JR . . .

After meeting Sgt. Libby, I was very excited for many veterans that I knew to also meet him to share their service stories. I always enjoy the conversation between them and cherish that educational moment. John Esposito was no exception to the conversations that I wished to hear.

My Uncle John, served here in the states as well as overseas in north Africa with the US Air Force from 1957 – 1960 and was also in the US Army. He received the National Defense Service Medal and Good Conduct Medal during his time in the Air Force.

Uncle John was quite the boxer, becoming a champion in his weight class and eventually going pro after the service with only 1 loss in his over 75 fights that he had under his belt, with most of his wins being knockouts. This was the majority of the conversation with Sgt. Libby as they each shared about how they liked the service, the hardships they faced and how each of them stayed in great shape. Another outward demonstration of how proud each one of them were to have served this great country and to have always been ready for whatever was thrown at them.

Sgt. Libby remembers my uncle as well from his performances of impersonating Elvis Presley and the great shows that he put on for the public in his later years of life.

In 2016, my uncle, John Esposito, passed away but not without leaving his legacy and being honored by the Korean War Veterans who honored him with the rifle salute at his funeral and a proper military style funeral to honor this veteran. RIP Uncle John, you are truly missed.

JOSEPH DIBLIN . . .

Our friend Barb Spaventa introduced us after I met her at a book signing. She knew that we all had to meet and share stories. . . *She was right!* Meeting this man was extraordinary to say the least. It started out as an interview about our book for a column that this WWII veteran still writes weekly for a local newspaper at 100 years old. The interview quickly turned into *me* asking *him* just as many questions about his interesting service. Conversation between the two WWII veterans was a great treat for me to witness and I can't think of a time when I felt more in touch with the feelings of the men who supported one another in two different parts of the world, yet each playing such a vital role that tied the two together.

A resident of Northumberland, PA, Joe had an amazing military career here in the US as a top test pilot. Joe was the pilot who could either make or break a plane's active service for others to fly in combat. The story goes that Joe was the pilot that found out what was causing a valuable airplane to catch on fire and crash that killed many others while Joe managed to solve the mystery mid-air and land the crippled plane for it to be examined, fixed and placed into service for the war effort.

Joe flew notable people from base to base as he was hand picked to do so due to his experience and many certifications. According to Joe himself, he qualified in over 100 different aircraft and logged in thousands of hours of flying them.

Joe is an amazing man and is one of the unsung heroes of WWII that once again, has his roots in Pennsylvania. Thank you Joe for all you did for our country and all you continue to do through your writing and many speeches you bless others with about our proud military history.

ERWIN SCHEUNEMANN . . .

Born 1929, US Navy Veteran on the USS Wright from 1950-1954. These years of the Korean conflict were considered *cold war era* and the Russians were at the top of our list to keep an eye on. 2nd class electrician mate, Erwin Scheunemann, spent his time on this vessel maintaining the electrical systems of this massive sub-hunter / killer which had a 750 foot emergency airfield deck for planes to land taking off from the USS Roosevelt and the USS Midway, who were in close proximity of the Wright.

I started out at The Great Lakes Naval Training Center and then off to Class A School for 16 weeks. I'd been fishing on boats before, but never on something so large! I really didn't get sea sick, but needed to go above the first couple of days to get some fresh air and then I'd feel much better . . . E. Scheunemann

Being an electrician / striker meant that you were able to work with a 1st class worker and were able to be exposed to more privileged information about the in's and out's of the ship, especially crucial for an electrician to strive for as they are responsible for the many inner-workings of this important vessel of the fleet.

After getting assigned and onto the ship, it was off to Port Smith for more training in dry dock on fire fighting and other important functions that they were required to have. From there, it was off to Cuba for the ship to get necessary repairs and checked out and then back to New York's Hudson Harbor before their trip to the Mediterranean Sea. This one month trip was a training session for the men along with other squadrons.

I got to go ashore and tour the Vatican and also got to see Monte Carlo while we were there. That was a big treat and it was very interesting for me . . . E. Scheunemann

Scotland was the next stop for young Erwin where they linked up with a British Carrier and four big Naval destroyers.

On this trip I became, along with all the other mates, a blue nose. This meant that we crossed the Arctic Circle. They gave us a little button that we wore on our uniform. I figured out were we were by the use of maps and showed the division officer and he commented that it was classified information and from then on I kept my mouth shut about it to the others. No planes could take off and they were all tied securely to the deck as was everything else on the ship as the waves would sometimes reach over 30 feet high. It was cold and the seas were very rough. We moved straight through them without any turns due to our capabilities and the angle that a ship is able to take before basically tipping over into the seas. For two weeks we spent our time performing our required tasks while divers tapped into vital telephone lines and installed transmitters to be able to listen to Russian radio transmissions. They listened and gave it all to the translators. We never knew what was going on but knew that it was very important to the US to get these transmissions . . . E. Scheunemann

I asked Erwin if there were any WWII military men on his ship that he met since it was so close to the dates of the end of the second world war and he responded . . .

There were a few of them on the ship. They were with us for about one year and offered us a lot of training. They shared their experiences and it was great to train with them . . . E. Scheunemann

Erwin's continued travels took him to the Gulf of Mexico for gunner training, the Atlantic to search for more subs, back to Cuba for atomic drills, back to New York and then back to Scotland for a second time. When his time was up, they asked him if he would like to re-up, go to the Pacific around Japan and get his next promotion to 1st class upon completion of his training, but he had other plans.

I enjoyed the four years. It was like a vacation to me and I learned a lot. It was interesting and I was proud to have served my country. I had a fiance waiting for me in Florida who I wanted to spend my time with. We eventually got married and that was the end of my military career . . . E. Scheunemann

We have met many veterans since our first book was released. Many get a book, read it, tell us good job or just say thank you for what you are doing. Erwin was a little different to me and I found it noteworthy to write about him as well as tell about the phone calls to me as he read the book *From The Command Car.*

He made sure to call as he completed his reading for the day. He indicated that it was very hard for him to put the book down because he was enjoying it so much. Day two, he told me that he would be reading later that night and that he would call me tomorrow. When I got the call the next day, I could hear a crackling in his voice from his emotions. He shared with me that the section about the *Letter of Protection* was especially heart-warming and touching to him on many levels as a reader, as a veteran as well as a Christian man. I myself was so touched about his love of the book and his sharing his feelings that I immediately called Sgt. Libby to share it with him and asked if he would like to go to meet Erwin so that they could shake hands and exchange stories. He agreed and the meeting was set up that day. The two men met in Danville, Pa and sat for a few hours as they spoke of their service and enjoyed each others company. I soaked up the moment and enjoyed it very much. Sgt. Libby presented Erwin with his very own *Letter of Protection* which meant a great deal to Erwin. The two men posed for photos, shook hands and left friends with a common bond. They both gave to their country and both shared a faith that stretches far beyond the uniform of a soldier, the faith that The Lord protected them both in their most dangerous moments in life.

God Bless you Erwin Scheunemann and thank you for your service to our great country. I am very proud to call you my good friend. My entire family loves you and thanks you for the great memories that we have shared together over these past few years. You are a special person to many.

FRED AGNONI . . .

Korean War veteran, Freddie is always there to help out at military events, especially driving his red Mustang in parades. A member of the Korean War Veterans Association in Williamsport, PA, Freddie attends meetings, funerals, parades and all types of veteran functions.

Fred also happens to be my second cousin on my mother's side of the family, so I have a special attachment to all of his war stories he tells. Freddie will also appear in a future release I am currently working on along with other Italian Americans about their service during the time of the Korean War.

He is also mentioned in a book written by Col. Cameron Adamson, a veteran of WWII, Korea and Vietnam! Col. Adamson's book was limited print and was only available to certain people, but Freddie is quick to show it to the many who are fans of this type of reading.

Fred drove Sgt. Libby as the Grand Marshall in a parade in Muncy, PA. He quickly agreed to be his driver and the two of them shared many stories about their time serving during their respective wars. I remember Fred looking at Mr. Libby and telling him that he served in Korea. Mr. Libby looked at him and in a solemn voice said, "*You guys had it rough there too.*" I myself knew that this was a compliment to Fred for what he had done and been through. The bond was formed and the two enjoyed the rest of the day together traveling in that bright red Mustang sports car, each waiving to the eager onlookers. God Bless You Freddie and thank you for your service and continued contributions to our country and it's veterans.

JOHN P. IRWIN . . .

WWII veteran, John is the author of the book *Another River, Another Town.* This meeting for me took place in Lewisburg, PA and it was by happenstance that I had mentioned my book to him. His wife quickly responded that he himself had written a book about his war experience and it was available on Amazon as well.

The first thing I did when I got home was to research it and order a copy. When it arrived, I began to read it and could not put it down! In my opinion, it is one of the best pieces of WWII history and exciting books that I have ever read! I could not wait to meet with him again and tell him just how much I loved his book. I usually don't have time to read a book a second time, bu with this one, it will be read *many more times.*

When I made the trip to visit him again, I made sure that I had his book in hand and a copy of mine to present to him. I sat for quite sometime and let him know how much I appreciated his service and how much I loved his book. I also mentioned that along with *From The Command Car,* they should both be movies for the theaters, NOW! He responded with thanks and a big smile saying, *"Do you really think so? I didn't think that anyone would still read my book."* Again, with praise and with eagerness to have him sign my copy, I assured him that it was a great book and that I was awestruck over what he had done during WWII. I also mentioned that I wished that I had helped him to write it.

I could not wait until I could get the two of these tank men togeth-er. Seems as if John was just ahead of Sgt Libby in most of the action and shares very similar memories of their time spent in the European Theater of Operations. The meeting was arranged, the two met and sat sharing many stories. I could tell at the end of the meeting when it was time for us to leave that the two did not want to part ways. It was a very touching moment and I will cherish it forever.

God Bless you John and once again, thank you for your service and our newly formed friendship. I look forward to hearing many more stories from this American hero in the future!

GEORGE DEFFENBAUGH . . .

United States Air Force Master Sgt. and continued supporter of veterans and their families for many years. George was an airplane fabricator and also fixed many planes after they were as he would say, *"shot up!"* Grand Marshall at parades and led his own small branch of The American Legion which met at an assisted living facility in the Williamsport area. His love for God family and country was most evident.

We became great friends and the more military events that I was invited to, Sgt. Libby and Master Sgt. Deffenbaugh became friends and shared the spotlight often! They would exchange stories and always left one-another with a firm handshake and a big smile. George passed away in 2016 and is missed by many of his legion friends, loving family and all those who knew and loved this great man! I spoke at his funeral at the request of his family and paid tribute to his many talents, his love for his family and his sense of humor. It was an honor to be a part of his final tribute.

His love for music and attention to it's detail still is a reminder to me each time I perform with his words always in my mind, *"You have a good show for us today?"* As if he was prompting me to remember that all of my shows must be top notch, he would smile and take his seat close by to close his eyes and enjoy each note I sang. RIP my friend, God Bless you for all you gave your country.

Others to mention for their interaction with Sgt.. Libby at events, their friendships and their honorable service include . . .

Denny Bennett, Kevin Bittenbender, Mickey Yonkovig – WWII radar operator, Charles Brooking – WWII Pontoon Boat Operator, Dick Donald – WWII Iwo Jima.

The many serving soldiers and veterans that we have met are all important and deserve recognition. Our apologies to those we may have missed. God Bless you all and we hope to see you again at a future event. God bless America!

SPECIAL AUTHOR DEDICATION

I first became aware of the service of our great men and women from the service of my grandfather, **Charles E. Hunter.** My grandfather spoke of his service and that of his brother **William E. Hunter.** I was young and did not ask all that I would love to know now, but knew I was proud to say that my *pop pop* was in the US Army!

My grandfather and Sgt. Libby were born in the same city and in the same year, only 1 month apart. They lived near one-another and may have met but Sgt. Libby's recollection of him is fuzzy.

```
The name sounds familiar and I knew some
Hunter's, but that was so long ago it is
kind of fuzzy to me . . . C. Libby
```

My grandfather was a railroader and served in that capacity in his later service, running men and supplies to the camps across the Eastern section of the country. He was preparing to ship over to Europe to serve in the same capacity when the armistice was signed and was not sent over. His railroading continued for over twenty years and our entire family is proud of him.

Private First Class Charles E. Hunter of the 109th Infantry.
Photos circa 1940's, unknown photographer.

That's A Wrap!

* * *

AS THEY SAY IN SHOW business, *"That's a wrap!"* In wrapping up this *bookend* writing project if you will, I wonder what types of conclusions as a reader and enthusiast of American history have come to. As you finish this record of a person's life that has not only reached a magnificent milestone, but that has seen the horrors of war up close and personal, what have you concluded? To further your examination, I'd like to share with you some personal insight that I have seen and heard from the great man that I have had the privilege of writing about now in two books. Little things that I have picked up and noticed through these ten years of knowing him and calling him my friend. Enjoy these little tid- bits of information that will give you as a reader a more in depth view of his personality and his inner thoughts and more importantly, his kindred spirit.

Telephone calls . . . A telephone call from Sgt. Libby is what I refer to as an *event*! You *never know* what you are going to hear or talk about when you pick up the phone. The caller ID announces, *"Call from, Libby Charles"* and immediately, your curiosity becomes charged. As you pick up the telephone, you better be ready for anything and I do mean, anything! At times there is no regulator or gate to stop some of the things that come out of his mouth. I say this tongue and cheek, but at 100 years old, I think that if he is thinking something, he *needs* to say it, no matter what others may think. It is almost as if it is a combination of needing to vent to someone that does not judge him like myself or needing to say it do that I can document what he is thinking either for the book itself or for my own knowledge and overall betterment.

A telephone call at 6:30 AM is not an uncommon thing when we are deep into our writing. I figure that the military years and the fact that he has been an early riser as a hunter, in his mind tells him that I should be up as well. A firm voice after I answer, "*Steve, this is Charlie*" rings into my ears. As quickly as I reply, it's right to the point of the call, no beating around the bush. At the start of the writing process on book # 1, I instructed him to call anytime he thought of a good story or something that would help me in the writing process. Sometimes, we can finish speaking on a topic and the phone will ring again, not five minutes later. I smile and get ready for the next barrage of information that got stirred up from our last topic of conversation.

Voice mail is another event with Sgt. Libby. I have received a multitude of messages from new stories to getting chewed out to asking about my health to warnings about the pending bad weather. All interesting and all from the heart of a caring man. I have started to preserve many of them on a cassette tape to have for the day that the voice mails themselves stop. I had inadvertently saved a few on my voice mail account and after losing my own father, found one from him. I cherish this father's day message that I had saved from him that previous year. In my moments of needing to hear the voice of my father, I can push play and hear his voice while spiritually connecting with him for that short moment. Listening to those few words in his own voice comforts me and helps me through those moments of loss. I hope that in the pages of this book, there may be many ways for readers to remember their family members and all of the stories that should not be forgotten in the life that they lived while here on earth.

I always end my conversation with Sgt. Libby by saying to him, "*I love ya Mr. Libby, God Bless You!*" I am always reminded about how short life is and what his age is and want for my last spoken words to him to always be these.

He always responds, *"Bye now, same to you."* I end each telephone call with a smile and a slight lump in my throat thinking about the days that I will not be able to hear him say those words to me. God has a way of placing special people into your life that make a difference and an impact on you. God gave me a very special one when he gave me Mr. Libby to call my friend, my adopted dad / grandfather and I thank God each and every day for that very special blessing. Even the phone calls at 6:30 AM.

Sound Effects . . . When a person tells a story that they are passionate about, they usually have their signature way of telling the story by adding certain accents, hand gestures, facial expressions or raising the volume or tone of their voice. In the case of Sgt. Libby, when you hear a story, you get a variety of wartime sound effects. You get the sound of a burp gun firing or the sound that an armor- piercing shell sounds as it comes out of the tank. You also hear the sounds of a German fighter pilot's machine gun fire as it hits the ground as well as the unique sounds of the V-1 or V-2 bombs that the Germans used against our troops during the war.

```
When you hear artillery sounds around you,
the incoming German ones sounded broken up
and not smooth. You knew they were coming
toward you and you took cover. The outgoing
shells from our guns sounded very smooth
and much quieter than the German ones. We
would say to each other, there's the outgo-
ing mail or take cover, here's the incoming
mail . . . C. Libby
```

His whistle is still sharp and can throw a call for quite a distance. He can mimic the sounds of all he heard while in battle and uses them accordingly during his speeches. With hands motioning where the bullets hit around his body from the German fighter plane and imitating the sounds of the bullets hitting the ground, his story becomes even more enthralling to witness.

The sounds of the V-1 and V-2 bombs are also interesting to hear him mimic. He often explains that when you heard that sound, they were instructed to open their mouths to prevent the pressure from doing damage to their ear drums.

The sounds of the different vehicles are also in his repertoire. From the sounds of his command car to the sounds of the different tanks, he paid attention and locked in the many sounds that would alert him and that helped to save his life on many different occasions.

Studying someone's mannerisms and personality . . . As a person gets older, you can imagine that they become a little more in touch with the way they feel about another person. They learn to watch for signals which indicate whether that person is telling the truth or is nervous about what they are saying. Your internal radar picks up on many of these mannerisms or personality traits in order to properly evaluate your safety or your ability to interact in a relaxed manner with them.

Sgt. Libby has a keen sense of reading others and often shares these findings with me. I do remember in many conversations, the interrogations of German soldiers that he took part in. Questions to them were always firm and to the point. They had to quickly determine if they were lying or if they had something they were hiding from them that could harm others within their unit.

Today, Sgt. Libby uses a more subtle form of interrogation and looks into the person's eyes to see all he can. He watched their mannerisms while talking and interacting. He reads others like they are telling him just what they are feeling and thinking and is usually spot on.

On the dance floor, he can spot a woman that is uncomfortable or sad that she is not dancing or has not been asked to dance. He can read their body language on the floor as to what style of dance he should incorporate as to not offend her or to cause her to stumble in her steps. All from his time of having to be completely on his game during WWII to protect himself as well as the other men on his vehicle.

What a gift to have and what a way to be able to weed out the people that would cause him any type of grief during the short amount of time that he has remaining here on earth. So, when talking to Sgt. Libby at a speech or a book signing, beware of his scanning and questioning. Relax, smile and let him do most of the talking and for goodness sake, don't interrupt him, pay attention to what he says! **Getting mad at someone** . . . Make no mistakes about this, even at 100 years old, this man is still in charge! He is still in charge of the family, he is still in charge of himself and he is certainly in charge of how I am to write this book. I enjoy when he gets a little worked up and you can tell that he is aggravated. The common statement out of his mouth is, *"Don't get my Irish up!"* This meant that his Irish blood was starting to boil and you better not cross the line. Time to back off, change the subject or quickly apologize for what you said or did. I honestly think that he could still kick someone's tail in a fist fight! I have even heard him telling someone that he would punch them in the mouth for what they said. I love that *tough-as-nails* spirit that he still has at 100 and hope that I have it with all of it's glory when I get up there in age.

Now with that said, Sgt. Libby is quick to self examine after he loses his temper. He is known to make a telephone call or to personally visit someone to say that he is sorry for what he either said or did. Integrity and compassion is in no shortage with this man, something that we should all take a long look at and life lesson from.

Helping others . . . Sgt. Libby has three living children that either live with him or very near him. It is all they can do to make sure that he paces himself and does not try to over do it with chores and simple tasks around his property. He still counts on them to aid in things that involve lifting and bigger projects, but wants to help out in any way he can to maintain his flexibility, his general strength and most of all, to help his children as often as he possibly can. Just the other day, he worked outside pushing a wheelbarrow for almost four hours as he cleaned up branches from a tree that his son had cut down the previous day, out there doing that by himself.

He is the same way with anyone that needs help. Many stories within our first book, he spoke to me about how he aided other soldiers, his family and complete strangers in their times of need. From helping stressed out on the verge of mental collapse soldiers to returning home to his mother and father from the CCC Camp to aid them in flood clean up to providing a dying girl with two different blood transfusions above and beyond the limit that they normally take from a single person without any type of complaints. This man has a heart of gold and will to this day help out in any way he can if the purpose is to make things better for that person.

During my recent recovery from surgery and after a long illness I suffered last year, he was sure to call and make sure that I didn't need anything. I had no doubt that this old command car driver would get into his newer vehicle and drive right over to my house to do anything he could to take care of me. It is just they way he thinks and wants to act as a Christian man and as a former soldier to serve others.

When The Endless Mountains War Museum asks Sgt. Libby to come and speak in the process of earning contributions for it's big expansion project. He never hesitates to accept and share his stories with the crowds. His kindness is felt by the entire crowd as he goes through each and every emotion of what he felt during his time in WWII. The crowd gets angry at the stories of the enemies, laughs at the more humorous events and tears up when he speaks of the fallen comrades of the 628th and many units they were attached to in battle.

Once in service, always in service. With a heart as big as the tanks he escorted into battle, Sgt. Libby is surely a special type of person that is hard to find most anywhere in this world.

Being polite . . . One thing that sticks in my mind about Sgt. Libby is that he does not tolerate someone being rude. Many people that he knew back many years ago that still see him to this day, walk by him, don't say hello or turn their heads when he looks at them for a proper greeting. This bothers him so much that he can't wait to give me a call and tell me how rude they were. This truly worries him due to the fact that many of the youth he encounters also have no manners! If the adults do it, then what will the kids of this generation feel they should do when it comes to this important trait and quality of politeness within our society?

He'll give you the shirt off of his back if you need it without hesitation, but if you are rude and disrespectful, he would rather strangle you with that same shirt. His time spent in the military taught him that kindness and respect went a long way. His mother also instilled this into him at an early age and it has stuck with him to this very day. With a Bible in her hand, she taught him the values that are still woven within his very fiber of a man.

He has commented that troops treat each other with respect and that it transfers into how they watch out for one-another on the battlefield. His belief is that the civilian population should also act accordingly and take a lesson from the military and how the boys within the CCC Camps were required and supposed to act toward others.

Sometimes at a speaking event, there will be that one person that abuses the *does anyone have a question to ask* segment. I can see him want to move onto another person to give equal time, but he still remains very polite and allows them to ramble on until I put a stop to it and change the subject or start a new segment to help the presentation flow. All the while, a smile on his face and making sure that he stays focused on telling his stories. A slight whisper in my ear may contain the comment, *"Shut this guy up, will ya?"* But all the time understanding that many want to also share their personal family stories with him.

When it comes to the ladies . . . now we are talking politeness and excellent manners. Opening the door, calling her miss or ma'am, allowing her to speak first, escorting her back to her chair, making sure that she feels comfortable and many other customs that are associated with treating a woman with respect and using proper manners. Many of these are a fading example of the faster, more abrupt, rude society that we now live in. He would never think of having his face in the screen of a cell phone or checking e-mails while another person is talking to him. He would never allow another person to speak in a rude manner to a woman in his presence. He would also never make an advance to a woman that was not appropriate and without consent, all a sign of his true character and upbringing from a young child. Take a lesson from this man and try to reverse this ever-changing lack of both respect for others and lack of self-respect that is taking over this present younger generation.

Dressing like a gentleman . . . To Sgt. Libby, being a gentleman and having integrity are two of the most important attributes that any man can carry with him through life. The way a man dresses is also very important and he believes that it is a symbol of your inner-most personality and your sign of self-worth.

One of the most commented things that I hear from him in reference to what the officers had said to him is that he always looked like a soldier and conducted himself like a gentleman. This is one of his most important accomplishments and he still follows that rule today. What a joy to have yet a person that still after all these years of being out of the military, to still want to conduct himself like a soldier with pride and tradition. He keeps himself fit, he keeps active and he still expects to be looked at in the same way he did when he was young and serving within the armed forces.

So, take some advice from myself and Sgt. Libby . . . *Pull your pants up!* and buy a belt, turn your hat forward the way it was intended to be worn, tie your shoes and stop sticking metal objects all over you face! People will treat you differently as you treat yourself with self respect. Don't cry and whine that you don't get respect when you present yourself like a person who does not deserve it in the first place.

One time we did a book signing and speech where he wore his WWII hat. He loves wearing his uniform and hat to show just exactly what war he fought in and how he can still fit into his uniform. He is very particular about keeping track of all his personal items, especially when it comes to this.

On that particular day, he had worn a jacket due to it being a little cold outside. When we sat in our spot prior to the presentation, I helped him remove his jacket and for some odd reason that day, he removed his hat. Not to lose track of it or have it disappear while we were preoccupied, I slipped it into the sleeve of his jacket to keep it safe.

A wonderful presentation, autographs signed and everyone happy, Sgt. Libby slipped his jacket on and we headed back down the road toward home. About fifteen minutes after we started driving, he started to panic asking me where his hat was. This caused me to get anxious as well and we started to recap where he may have left it. I ran the entire day through my head once more and recalled me helping him take off his jacket earlier that day. I started to chuckle a little and he asked me what was so funny. I reached over and felt the sleeve of his jacket and realized what had happened.

I said, Mr. Libby, why is one sleeve bigger than the other one? He looked and started laughing himself while pulling his hat out of his coat sleeve. It was a moment that we shared where the smallest little thing made him enjoy his time that much more. We still joke about that and recall it every time I help him with his jacket and hat.

Being on time . . . This is a *big* pet-peeve of Sgt. Libby that he is always on time for what he has committed to. It is an even *bigger* deal to him that *you* are on time and there when he requested you be there. It must be a military thing that has stuck with him all of these years.

At times, I have been a little behind schedule and I could tell that if I was wearing private stripes, the TEC5 Sgt. would be giving me extra guard duty or latrine cleanup or *both*! I have learned that I better be completely prepared for our meetings and get out the door extra early to avoid traffic hold-ups and try to arrive a little early. I never want for him to think that I don't appreciate the time spent with him, therefore, my advice to all of you is to never keep a soldier waiting and to be ready for whatever they have in their minds to be discussed or completed during that blessed visit.

When the day comes that Sgt. Libby is no longer with us, my conversations have ended and I feel that emptiness, I will surely remember his lessons and will include them into my regular routine of being prompt and respectful of anyone that is depending on me for anything. Thank you for the important life lessons Sgt. Libby.

Staying fit . . . Something that has always been important to this 100 year old man is staying fit. He now enjoys the freedom at this advanced age to still dance, do yard work, errands and chores around his house, hunt and drive himself to wherever he chooses to go.

While attending a party of a relative of Sgt. Libby during the writing of this book, I mentioned a few stories that I had fun writing. We got onto the subject of swimming and he shared this information with me about Sgt. Libby and how fit he has stayed. He told me that in Sgt. Libby's 80's, he would still do swan dives off of the family diving board into the pool, swim with the ability of someone much younger and would also do some tricks that many people have never been able to do. He witnessed Mr. Libby in a hand stand and then flip into a dive from the board. I thanked him for sharing this story and could not wait to share it with all of you as you begin to let everything sink in as to how remarkable this man has kept himself and possibly apply his lifestyle to yours to aid in the days that you yourself are approaching the milestone of 100 years.

As well as being fit, I myself have been scolded a time or two on a day that I didn't shave or if my hair had gotten a little too long or if I started to show a little too much belly growth. Taking care of yourself and showing pride is an important thing to Sgt. Libby and in his mind, through the lessons instilled in the CCC Camps and the US military, others should have this same mindset.

"That and a ham sandwich" . . . A line used to divert attention or to calm his embarrassment in a situation where he has received praise. With a smile and some quick witted humor, the line *"That and a ham sandwich"*, is something that I have grown fond of when with Sgt. Libby. I laugh and then reflect at the many popular sayings and word usages that have gone by the wayside in his long lifetime.

If you watch an old black and white detective movie or a WWII movie made during that time or even some of the 3 Stooges or Abbott and Costello flicks, you will hear many of these coined phrases that have all but disappeared from the regular vocabulary of Americans. Words that meant something back then don't mean the same now and phrases that applied to things that were going on in the news are unknown to this current generation of people. Another response when asking hi how he feels is a quick comeback of, *"Fat, ragged and sassy!"* A saying that he told me he made up himself. I love that one as well as my daughters who enjoy his vocabulary and sayings. I find myself struggling at times with a few of them, but quickly realize that I am speaking with a *walking history book*. A man that has seen so many changes within our society and the world for that matter, that I feel a responsibility to soak them all up and try to preserve them all for posterity purposes. What will it get me? I'm not really sure, but I'll enjoy them all . . . and *a ham sandwich*.

During the transferring of my notes to the manuscript, I would regularly call Sgt. Libby and talk to him about my ideas for the book and it's many forms of presentation. One idea that we want to do is to make an audio CD for people to listen to in their car or at home or for the blind to be able to hear these amazing stories. While I was talking about all the possibilities, I commented that his voice would be captured on audio for all the generations to hear, year after year after year. His comment was this,

> Well, you know that it may not be too many more
> years. People beating each other up, weath-
> er changing, the world getting crazy . . .
> C. Libby

I said, *"Are you referring to the return of The Lord?"* His comment was this.

> Why yes, it's not too far away. Get good
> with him and be ready. My mother told me
> once, Charles, there will be a day that the
> seasons will only be told by the color of
> the leaves. Things will get really bad. I
> believe that she was talking about right
> now! . . . C. Libby

I further asked him about his salvation and his relationship with The Lord and he offered this to me about the long life he has lived and his choices, good and bad.

> I hope that the good Lord forgives me for
> the bad things I have done in my life. I
> wasn't always perfect. I have had plenty
> of women in my life and I am sure that he
> wasn't happy about that. But, I guess that
> I've really tried to make up for that by
> asking for forgiveness and trying to always
> do the right things. It hit me one day that,

```
Charlie, you should give people that Letter
of Prayer and try to help them to believe
in the good Lord and how God will protect
them through his son Jesus Christ. So, I
went to the store and started getting them
copied to hand out to anyone that would
listen to me and believes in the words of
the letter. I tell them they can believe or
not, most ask if they can have one and a
few say they'll pass. That's their choice,
but I believe in the words and that is what
helped me stay alive all through the war
and even til today . . . C. Libby
```

So, the simple ministry of Charles A. Libby began. He knows that the piece of paper is not the magic item that will protect them. What he does know is that the words of the letter are a statement of faith in God and how we are not supposed to test him, but follow him and to always trust him. Wisdom from a man that has seen and witnessed so much and wisdom from a man that places his faith in a place called *Heaven*. My advice to my readers is to listen to this advice since nobody will know the time, the day, the month or the year of his return, *then* people, it's too late.

From The Author

* * *

Our days may come to seventy years, or eighty, if our strength endures; yet the best of them are but trouble and sorrow, for they quickly pass, and we fly away. If only we knew the power of your anger! Your wrath is as great as the fear that is your due. Teach us to number our days, that we may gain a heart of wisdom. Psalm 90 : 10-12

Photo taken of Hunter Family and Sgt. Charles Libby at his 100 Year Birthday Bash!.

100 Years of Stories has been such a joy for me as a writer to present to all of you. I started this project writing with enjoyment and pain alike as I use this down-time recovering from surgery to focus and keep myself from doing anything that may work against my healing process. Being a martial arts master, an avid outdoors man, a musical entertainer /singer / drummer, a speaker and all-around hard worker, it keeps me busy and as you can imagine. I am always at a high risk for injuries that can put you down for a few weeks if I am not careful enough. I can't get comfortable in my chair, my breaks are frequent and that disrupts my thought process and it sometimes takes several hours to get back into the mood and the flow of writing to proceed. Then I realize that I had the choice of having elective surgery. I had physicians working on me in a clearly lit operating room without bombs being dropped around us. My pain went away and I am 100% again. All of these things that I felt have passed, but for many that served in WWII and any other war that soldiers wore the uniform of The United States of America's bravest, many did not have the same luxury that I do at this particularly tough time in my life. Let's call it a road bump or a slight inconvenience to my active lifestyle, but by no means, is this close to what our soldiers had felt or still feel today when faced with pain of an injury on the battlefield or the fears of the next attack upon them and whether or not they will be one of the unfortunate ones that get hit with a chunk of lead or flaming hot metal soaring through the air at speeds unable to be seen by the human eye.

I struggle with the pains that I know will disappear physically and probably will not carry any mental scars that would preclude me from activity or sneak up on me when I least expect it. But for the soldier that suffered the horrors of war, they feel some form of pain each and every day. They are constantly reminded of their own injuries. They are triggered by events to remind them of what they saw, smelled, heard and felt as they witnessed their comrades being carried off of the battlefield, unable to walk off on their own. This book is not only a compilation of stories from the man who is Sgt. Charles A. Libby, but also a tribute to the men and women that fought before him, with him, now and those who will choose to or be forced to fight for our great country in the future!

Safe spaces, trophies for everyone, social acceptance of a person's weaknesses or alternative lifestyles with a rewarded type of normalcy has truly gotten out of hand. Punishing those who speak out to help make them become stronger as well as the ridicule and prosecution of those who make it a point to stand up for what we know as being normal is all too common and it all must end! It mocks what they as soldiers have done for us and belittles those of us who work hard to earn and receive what we have and have been recognized for!

More about author, Steve Hunter . . . Published articles can be researched under the following names : Shihan Steve Hunter, Shujin Sensei Steve Hunter, Soke Steve Hunter and Sensei Steve Hunter. All the many martial arts titles throughout the years during my writing process in magazines articles as well as newspaper columns.

Some of my published works can still be found online from my past writing if you are interested in reading where I started my love for this avenue of creativity. A newspaper column in The Woodlands Villager, near Houston, TX for nearly four years was a regular source of writing in the late 90's and early 2000's. Some of these articles are also available online for your reading pleasure and educational purposes.

My first book *Training Heroes — The martial arts training of a US Navy SEAL* is no longer on the market, but a second edition of the book with a similar title will be available on Amazon by early 2018. This chronicles the training that I provided as a martial arts instructor to the now famous twin brother SEAL warriors, Marcus and Morgan Luttrell. It is the true story that Hollywood *forgot* to tell in the top-selling movie, *The Lone Survivor.* Soon, you will all be able to read and understand the truth of how this SEAL and his brother both survived their many battles fought! This is a more personal piece of military history that I wish to preserve that I am both proud of and was truly an important part of.

From The Command Car is the first book that I wrote about the now famous WWII veteran and the follow up Sgt. Libby is a must for all readers to own! Check out : www.fromthecommandcar.com

To reach author Steve Hunter, send an e-mail to shihanhunter@yahoo.com. You can also visit his Facebook pages at From The Command Car or Shihan Steve Hunter.

Private Libby of the 109th Infantry prior to his joining the 628th.
Photos circa 1940's, unknown photographer.

Sponsors of History

✳ ✳ ✳

THANK YOU . . . TO THE MANY sponsors that have helped with the start-up financial donations to make this book possible. Also, to the many people, groups and organizations that have helped to spread the word and sponsor events for *From The Command Car* and that committed to more events for this newest publication. I would like to dedicate this section to mentioning some of those who have participated in some form or fashion out of love and respect for this great man and war hero.

THE ENDLESS MOUNTAINS WAR MUSEUM
103 Main Street Sonestown, PA 17758
Jack Craft
Owner & preserver of historical war artifacts, Museum President

*In lieu of flowers or gifts, Sgt. Libby requests that monetary donations be made to this museum upon his death to aid in the preservation of these important artifacts of history. Each telling a particular story, Sgt. Libby found it very interesting to walk the many isles and displays at Endless Mountains during his many visits there to speak.

THE UNION COUNTY VETERANS 4TH OF JULY PARADE
Lewisburg, PA
Facebook : Union County Veterans' 4th of July Parade
info@unioncountyveterans4thofjuly.com

QUILTS OF VALOR FOUNDATION
www.qovf.org
Facebook : Quilts of Valor Foundation

THE NIPPENOSE VALLEY VILLAGE
www.nippenosevalleyvillage.com
Facebook : Nippenose Valley Village – A Senior Living Community
Owners : Julie Steinbacher, Chris Larson and Troy Musser
Director of Admissions & Marketing Director : Virla Ocker

THE BRASS PELICAN RESTAURANT
1119 Elk Grove Rd.   Benton, PA 17814
Big supporters of Pennsylvania History and Heritage –
Owner : Monica Diltz
Benton, Pennsylvania's BEST home cooking and meeting spot!

LYCOMING HOW " HELPING OUR WARRIORS "
Facebook : Lycoming County Helping Our Warriors
Donations mailed to : Lycoming HOW
29 Lehman Dr.   Cogan Station, PA 17728
Patricia Cohick

Special Thanks . . .
to the following people, organizations and companies for their generosity . . .

Representative Jeff Wheeland & Family . . . Supporters of our military and their families.

Carol Evans & Family . . . Niece of Sgt. Libby, preserving their rich family heritage.

Barbara Spaventa & Family . . . Active and proud participant in veteran affairs and awareness.

Ruth N. Rode . . . South Williamsport, PA. Great supporter of our history in PA and beyond!

Rennie Rodarmel Agency . . . Allstate Insurance Company located in Williamsport, PA

Denny Bennett . . . South Williamsport, PA, Retired US Army 1st Sgt. Proud Veteran!

Todd & Julia Lehman . . . Active and proud participants in veteran affairs and awareness.

Hudock Capital Group, LLC . . . Supporters of our military. Located in Williamsport, PA

Machmer Chiropractic and The Machmer Family . . . Williamsport, PA *SPECIAL thanks for the scanner during the photo portion of this project!

Reading Recommendations

* * *

FOR YOUR READING PLEASURE AND to further your education in our rich American military history, I would like to recommend these wonderful and informative publications to purchase and enjoy.

From The Command Car by Steve Hunter **ISBN # - 9780692512418**

Another River, Another Town by John P. Irwin **ISBN # - 0-375-50775-2**

Remembering Firebase Ripcord by Christopher J. Brady **ISBN # - 978-1-4787-6178-5**

Beyond The Wall by Alivia Tagliaferri **ISBN # - 978-0-9788417-2-0**

AUTHOR PHOTO CREDIT
Special thanks to Danny Irimagha for his professionalism and talents! Find him on Facebook.

A photo from one of our first book signings together.
Tivoli, PA *Photo 2016, photographer Alma Hunter.*

Made in the USA
Middletown, DE
23 January 2018